the simple guide to PUPPIES

Stacy Kennedy

T.F.H. Publications, Inc.

T.F.H. Publications, Inc.
One TFH Plaza
Third and Union Avenues
Neptune City, NJ 07753

www.tfhpublications.com

Contents

Part One—Starting Out . . . . **.9**

Chapter 1: Should You Get a Puppy? 11

    Puppy Time 12

    Home, Sweet Home 14

    The New Roommate .16

    Looking Good 17

    How Much Fun Can You Take? 18

Chapter 2: Which Puppy Is Right for You? 21

    The Purebred Dog 22

    The Mixed Breed 30

Chapter 3: Where to Look for Your Puppy 33

    Finding a Breeder 33

    Shelters 36

    Rescue 38

Chapter 4: Selecting a Healthy Puppy—From Head to Toe 39

Temperament Testing 40

How to Interpret the Scores 46

In Conclusion 48

Chapter 5: Getting Prepared 49

Veterinary Care 49

License to Own 50

Preparing for Your Puppy 50

Settling In 55

Puppy-Proofing Your Home 55

Preparing Your Family 60

Chapter 6: Puppy Comes Home 63

Leaving the Breeder 64

The First Few Days 68

Chapter 7: Understanding Your Puppy 71

Pack Mentality 71

How Puppies Develop 73

The Newborn Puppy 73

The Next Four Weeks 74

Leaving Home 76

Growing Up 77

The Terrible Teens 78

Canine Behavior 80

Understanding the Dog's Language 81

First
Night
Page 67

Puppy Socialization 82

How to Socialize Your Dog 83

Starting Over 85

Forming a Bond 87

Part Two—Your Healthy Puppy **91**

Chapter 8: Health Care 93

How to Recognize a Healthy Puppy 93

Veterinary Care 94

The First Checkup 95

Canine Diseases 97

External Parasites 100

Intestinal Parasites 103

Heartworm Disease 105

Spaying and Neutering 105

Recognizing Trouble 107

Giving Medication 110

Dental Care 111

Chapter 9: Puppy First Aid 115

Cardiac Arrest 116

Bleeding 116

Shock 117

Choking 117

Drowning 118

Heatstroke 118

Poisoning 119

Seizure 119

Accidents 120

Electrocution 121

Walks on the Wild Side 121

Dog
Bites
Page 121

Chapter 10: Feeding and Nutrition 123

A Puppy's Nutritional Needs 123

Dog Foods 127

Good Food for Good Health 127

Types of Dog Food 129

Reading Labels 129

Homemade Diets 132

Feeding Your Puppy 133

Treats and Bones 137

Chapter 11: Grooming Your Puppy 139

Coat Types 140

The Road to Beauty 142

Part Three—Training 149

Chapter 12: Housetraining Your Puppy .151

Potty Training 152

Crate Training 154

Outside Schedule 156

Accidents Will Happen 160

Chapter 13: Basic Training for Good Behavior 161

The Right to Be Trained 161

Why Is Training Important? 162

Professional Training 163

Training Methods 163

Finding an Instructor or Trainer 165

Collar and Leash Training .166

Household
Rules

Page 153

Puppy Kindergarten 167

Basic Commands 167

Problem Solving 177

The Canine Good Citizen® Test 187

Part Four—Having Fun **191**

Chapter 14: Traveling With Your Dog 193

Road Trips 193

On Your Way 197

Air Travel 198

Leaving Your Puppy Behind 199

Chapter 15: The Ambitious Puppy 203

Activities and Service 203

Carting and Draft Dogs 205

Therapy Dogs 205

Assistance Dogs 206

Search and Rescue Dogs 206

Chapter 16: Organized Dog Sports and Events 209

Conformation 209

Junior Showmanship 212

Obedience 213

Tracking 214

Agility 215

Flyball 216

Frisbee™ 217

Preparing
for Flight
Page 196

Earthdog Trials 218

Field Events 219

Herding Trials 221

Lure Coursing 222

Resources 223

Index 227

Part One
Starting Out

Should You Get a Puppy?

So, you are thinking about getting a puppy. Dog ownership is a big step, bigger than most people realize. That adorable little puppy you bring home will mature to become a fully-grown adult and will most likely be a member of your family for 12 to 15 years, perhaps even longer.

You will be responsible for your pet's well-being for quite some time. You will also be responsible for training your dog to become well-adjusted and polite, a pleasure to own, and an asset to the neighborhood. You will have to feed, exercise, groom, and keep your pup safe and

The decision to own a dog requires a great deal of thought and planning.

Dogs have been shown to lower stress and improve quality of life.

Your new puppy will need lots of love and attention.

healthy for life. If it sounds like a major commitment, it is. Most people do not consider the extent of commitment that dog ownership entails before picking up the first adorable pup they see.

But puppy ownership can be a joy as well. The fulfillment that you receive watching your pup grow and learn is incomparable, as is experiencing the love and affection that a dog gives back in return. Studies have shown that dogs can lower stress, help keep you fit, provide companionship, elicit laughter, and generally improve the quality of your life. By evaluating your needs first and then finding a puppy who best matches those needs, you can ensure that the dog you pick will fit perfectly with your family. Take the time to ask yourself and your family some questions about your lifestyle and what you all want to see in a dog. Then do your research. When you find the "perfect" puppy who will be your companion for life, you'll be glad you did.

Puppy Time

Puppies are like babies; they are absolutely adorable but also pretty helpless. Bringing an eight-week-old puppy into your home is almost like bringing a newborn home from the hospital: The "baby" will need your utmost attention and time until you both settle into a routine. For a few days, the puppy might be a little scared and lonely without the company of his mom and littermates. The pup will need extra attention and assurance until these new surroundings become familiar.

You will need to establish a schedule for eating, drinking, and outdoor time. Housetraining depends on a schedule. Puppies need to be taken to their potty area every few hours until they are at least 16 weeks of age (older for females), at which time they have better control of their bodily functions. They also need to go potty after eating, drinking, napping, and playing, as well as first thing in the morning and last thing at night.

Once housetrained, your puppy will still need to go outside at **least** three times a day, as well as get regular exercise to burn off all of that exuberant puppy energy. You'll need to spend time training; at first, to teach your puppy the household rules, and then good manners and basic obedience. You'll also need to spend time on grooming and on socializing him by going places, meeting people, and adjusting to different situations. That's a lot of time you'll need to spend with your new addition.

If you work ten-hour days or travel a lot and no one else is home to care for the dog, there is no way you will be able to give your puppy

Housetraining success depends on a regular outdoor schedule.

Did You Know That ...

Many communities in the US have breed-specific laws regarding dog ownership, usually directed toward breeds like Pit Bull Terriers, Rottweilers, or German Shepherd Dogs, making it illegal to own them. Although it may seem unfair to condemn a whole breed for what was probably a specific incident (often a dog bite or attack), it is important to know the laws of your community before getting a puppy.

The amount of space you can provide will determine the best dog for you.

Dogs need space to play, grow, and exercise.

enough attention. This is completely unfair and will result in an unhappy and destructive puppy, which, in turn, will make your life miserable. Be fair—if you and your family do not have the time to spend, don't bring a puppy into your life!

Home, Sweet Home

Dogs, even small ones, need space—space to play, grow, exercise, and be alone when they want. The amount of space you can provide will determine what kind of dog is best for you—or help you to rethink dog ownership.

First, there are basic considerations: Are you allowed to have a dog in your residence? If you rent your home or apartment or live in restricted housing like a condominium complex or retirement village, you may not be permitted to have a dog. Check your lease or your community by-laws to confirm that dogs are allowed in your home before investing your time and money in a puppy.

If you are permitted to have a dog or if you own your residence, take inventory of the space available. If you live in an apartment or condo, make sure that it is possible for you to take your puppy out for frequent walks and potty breaks. If your dog has access to a yard, is that yard fenced? Will your dog have unlimited access to the yard or will you need to build a dog run? Remember that your well-tended garden can be dug up in no time by an industrious young puppy who wants to

Coat Types

Curly or Short, Wavy Coats	Wire Coats	Long Coats	Silky Coats	Smooth Coats	Short Coats
Poodles	Most Terriers	Rough Collies	Afghan Hounds	Doberman Pinschers	Labrador Retrievers
Irish Water Spaniels	All Schnauzers	Australian Shepherds	Yorkshire Terriers	Boxers	German Shepherd Dogs
Kerry Blue Terriers		Shetland Sheepdogs	Irish, English, and Gordon Setters	Great Danes	
				Beagles	Welsh Corgis (Pembroke and Cardigan)
Portuguese Water Dogs		Lhasa Apsos		Basset Hounds	
		Most Spaniels		Dalmatians	

help you plant the spring flower beds. Building your puppy a dog run or designated area to use may be the best way to keep your yard looking nice. All of these things need to be considered before you bring a new puppy home.

Consider the size of your residence. A giant breed like a Great Dane or a Saint Bernard will not be happy or comfortable in a three-room apartment, and a little dog may feel overwhelmed with free access to a large house. Choose a puppy who will "fit in" best, especially when he is a full-sized adult.

What about your furnishings? Although they don't do it intentionally, puppies can be destructive. No matter how careful you are about trying to prevent it, little puppy

The breed of dog you choose will depend on the dynamics of your household.

Most family situations can accommodate a puppy.

teeth often find their way onto table legs and through couch cushions. Puppies will also have accidents on nice rugs, spill water on floors, and track mud through hallways. If a pristine house is really important to you, then you might think twice before getting a puppy.

The New Roommate

As previously stated, one of the most important factors to consider before choosing a puppy is the opinions of all the members of the household. Everyone who lives in your home must want a puppy. Even if you're sure you want a puppy to join the family, the type of dog you choose will be dependent on the dynamics of the household. There are all types of family situations and most can successfully raise a puppy. It's just a matter of finding the right puppy for each situation. Every dog, no matter what size, energy level, coat type, or exercise requirements, can find a family for a perfect fit.

For example, a senior couple may want to choose a puppy who will grow to be a small adult, one who can be easily handled and who may not need as much exercise as a larger dog. A household with small children may want a dog with a tolerant personality and good disposition, while a household with older children may want a dog who can match their high level of energy and play. A single person or couple with no children may want a dog who is more independent, rather than one who likes to run in packs. Some people may even consider getting two dogs to keep each other company.

It is important to research the different breeds as much as possible; get to know the breeds' personalities, talk to people who own them, and visit and play with the dogs before taking one home. Most dogs are placed in shelters because of behavior and training problems that could have been solved by better research beforehand and more time put into the training program. The more time and energy you put into finding the right dog, the more heartbreak you'll save yourself and your family. It is important to remember that, just as in human families, individuals within a breed are not all alike. Remember to evaluate the individual dog as well as the breed.

Looking Good

As dogs evolved through the ages, each group developed coats for protection from both the elements and predators. As dogs were selectively bred for certain purposes, their coats became matters of function. Dogs with short, smooth coats were good hunters because they didn't pick up burrs or become stuck in the field. Long coats helped dogs who were bred to work in colder climates stay warm. Through selective breeding by humans, dogs developed coats for specialized

Choose a breed that will fit your lifestyle.

Various coat types developed to protect against predators and the elements.

Different breeds will have different grooming requirements.

purposes, and although a good number of modern-day dogs are house pets, they still retain the coat that was best for their original function.

When you are choosing which breed of puppy you want, coat type is a very important consideration. Different breeds have different types of coats, and each will have specific grooming requirements. Don't get me wrong—every dog, purebred or mixed breed, needs regular grooming to stay healthy and look his best. But how regular is regular? Do you want to spend lots of time every day on grooming, or will your schedule only permit once a week? If you choose a breed that requires clipping, trimming, or stripping, are you willing to learn or would you rather pay someone to do it for you? Does shedding really bother you? The answers to these questions can be important factors when choosing a breed.

How Much Fun Can You Take?

All healthy puppies are playful, active, and full of energy. Puppies do grow up, however, and each breed will have certain exercise requirements that must be regularly met for its physical and mental well-being. If you pick the right puppy, the level of activity that both of you enjoy should be a perfect match throughout your life together.

What activities do you and your family participate in? Which of these activities can your dog join? The answers to these questions can play a big part in determining the

Healthy dogs are active and playful.

kind of dog you want. A jogger may want an active dog with a lot of stamina and energy. A swimmer or a boater may want a dog who loves the water. A hunter may want a dog to participate in field events. You may want to try your hand at obedience, agility, herding trials, earthdog events, lure coursing, flyball, or any other activities that you can do with your dog, or you may just want a dog who fits your mellow personality. If your idea of exercise is a couple of quick walks around the block, a short-legged Dachshund, a low-energy Bulldog, or a sauntering Saint Bernard may be the right breed for you. However, if you jog five miles every day and hike on the weekends, an active retriever or a high-energy Australian Shepherd or Border Collie may suit your needs.

The breed you choose should be suited to your activity level.

Picking the breed with the right activity level will keep both dog and owner happy. The right mix can be met to keep everyone involved (dog and human) physically and mentally fit. The dog's exercise needs will be met, which will keep your pet from becoming bored or overweight, and you will have a lifelong companion who is fun to take wherever you go. Remember, proper exercise will not only keep your dog looking good, it will keep you in shape as well.

Which Puppy Is Right for You?

Now that you've answered some important questions about your lifestyle, it's time to find out a little about what kinds of dog are out there. The answer is...plenty. There is literally a dog for every owner if you do your research. The best thing to do is narrow down the field to a few breeds that have the characteristics you find desirable, and then read as much about them as possible. There are many good, detailed books that give the histories and characteristics of each breed, as well as show pictures that illustrate exactly what the dog should look like. If you are interested in adopting a dog, read as much about the process

Beagle

Part 1

Golden Retrievers

The Eager Beavers

Some breeds want nothing more than to please their masters, while others just want to do as they please. The breeds most likely to want to make you happy and therefore train more easily are the Akita, Australian Shepherd, Border Collie, Doberman Pinscher, German Shepherd Dog, Golden Retriever, Standard Poodle, Rottweiler, Shetland Sheepdog, and the Welsh Corgi.

as possible. The better educated you are, the better your chances of finding the perfect puppy for you.

The Purebred Dog

There are certain advantages to choosing a purebred puppy. First, a purebred offers you a guarantee of what your puppy will look like as an adult–the size, coat type, activity level, and natural instincts have all been passed down from generation to generation. Second, because you are more likely to meet and observe the mother of your puppy, temperament can be better evaluated. When looking for a purebred dog of any breed, it is very important to find a responsible breeder who has been recommended by his or her national breed club. This way, you are assured that breeders will breed only the best dogs and that their dogs have been certified free of

Irish Setter

Sporting Group Breeds

24 to 50 pounds:	50 to 80 pounds:	
American Water Spaniel	Chesapeake Bay Retriever	Irish Setter
Brittany	Clumber Spaniel	Irish Water Spaniel
Cocker Spaniel (American)	Curly-Coated Retriever	Labrador Retriever
English Cocker Spaniel	English Setter	Pointer
English Springer Spaniel	Flat-Coated Retriever	Spinone Italiano
Field Spaniel	German Shorthaired Pointer	Vizsla
Nova Scotia Duck	German Wirehaired Pointer	Weimaraner
Tolling Retriever	Golden Retriever	Wirehaired Pointing Griffon
Sussex Spaniel	Gordon Setter	
Welsh Springer Spaniel		

certain heritable, genetic diseases. (How to find a breeder is discussed later in this book.)

If you want a purebred puppy but don't know what breed would be best for your family, try the dog breed selector test at www.selectsmart.com. This interactive Web site asks several questions and gives you a list of suitable breeds based on your answers. Another great Web site is Ralston Purina's breed selector at www.purina.com/dogs/index.html. This also prompts you through a series of questions and puts together a list of breeds that may be right for you. This site shows pictures of each breed and gives you information on size, activity level, trainability, temperament, and grooming requirements.

The American Kennel Club (AKC) recognizes 150 breeds of dog as of this printing, and there are over

Cocker Spaniel
(American)

Part 1

Labrador Retriever

Two sporting breeds were the most popular breeds in the US in 2003 AKC registrations: the Labrador Retriever was ranked 1st and the Golden Retriever was ranked 2nd.

400 breeds recognized worldwide. The breeds recognized by the AKC are divided into seven groups, which were derived from each breed's origin and purpose.

The Sporting Group

From the 1600s, sporting dogs have been developed to assist hunters in finding, pointing, flushing, holding, and retrieving game. Of the three types of sporting dogs—pointers, setters, and retrievers—many still perform the duties for which they were originally bred. Loyalty to their masters and trainability have helped them to become some of the most popular breeds for families. They have not been confined to using their skills just for hunting. These talented breeds also excel as therapy dogs, assistance dogs, and search and rescue dogs. Athletic and active, they are known for their good natures and enthusiastic attitudes, but they need plenty of exercise to keep their positive outlooks.

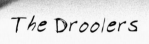

The Droolers

The worst offenders for dewy dewlaps are Newfoundlands, Saint Bernards, and Basset Hounds.

The Hound Group

There is little doubt that a hound-type dog was one of the earliest breeds that existed. Paintings on the walls of caves establish that hounds were used in ancient times to hunt animals. While times have changed and few hounds today are used for hunting purposes, this instinct remains strong in all the breeds in this group. The hounds are divided into two

Hound Group Breeds

Under 20 pounds:	50 to 80 pounds:	Over 80 pounds:
Dachshunds—Standard and Miniature	Afghan Hound	Bloodhound
20 to 50 pounds:	American Foxhound	Borzoi
Basenji	Black and Tan Coonhound	Irish Wolfhound
Basset Hound	English Foxhound	Otterhound
Beagle	Greyhound	Scottish Deerhound
Harrier	Ibizan Hound	
Norwegian Elkhound	Pharaoh Hound	
Petit Basset Griffon Vendéen	Rhodesian Ridgeback	
Whippet	Saluki	

subgroups: the sighthounds and the scenthounds, although the eyesight of the scenthound is excellent and the scenting ability of the sighthound is very keen. These hounds were selectively bred to hunt a wide variety of animals. Sighthounds, like the Scottish Deerhound and the Saluki, were used to find and chase down large game such as deer, elk, moose, and wild boar. Medium-sized hounds used both sight and scent for smaller game like rabbits and foxes. Small hounds, like Dachshunds, used scent to chase prey into the ground. The Hound Group is diversified; it includes both giant breeds and small breeds and is divided according to how the breed hunts.

Bloodhound

The most popular hound breeds in the US are the Beagle, ranked 3rd, and the Dachshund, ranked 5th, in 2003 AKC registrations.

Working Group Breeds

20 to 50 pounds:	Over 80 pounds:	
German Pinscher	Akita	Greater Swiss Mountain Dog
Portuguese Water Dog	Alaskan Malamute	Komondor
Standard Schnauzer	Anatolian Shepherd Dog	Kuvasz
50 to 80 pounds:	Bernese Mountain Dog	Mastiff
Boxer	Black Russian Terrier	Neapolitan Mastiff
Doberman Pinscher	Bullmastiff	Newfoundland
Giant Schnauzer	Great Dane	Rottweiler
Samoyed	Great Pyrenees	Saint Bernard
Siberian Husky		

Great Dane

The Working Group

All domestic dogs were once bred with the purpose of serving mankind, many breeds originally doing specific work for their masters. In every country, breeds were created to be draft dogs, hunters, and guardians. Many continue those duties today. The medium to very large breeds that make up the Working Group are well known for their athleticism, strength, courage, and loyalty—all attributes that have made them invaluable to the people who rely on them. Working dog enthusiasts have been concerned with retaining these breeds' versatility and function along with form. These breeds now often serve as police dogs, search and rescue dogs, therapy dogs, sled dogs, and draft dogs. Because of their large size and protective tendencies, they

The most popular working dog in the US is the Boxer, ranked 7th in 2003 AKC registrations.

need proper socialization and training, along with plenty of exercise. If you can provide a working dog with a job to do, you'll have an enthusiastic partner for life.

The Terrier Group

The name "terrier" is derived from the Latin word, terra, meaning earth; thus, the terrier is an earth dog. Terrier breeds come in all sizes. Developed specially to go to ground and burrow in the earth to chase and catch vermin like rats, foxes, badgers, weasels, and otters, the terrier was selectively bred for centuries to be a determined and tenacious dog. Long the companions of farmers, they also quickly endeared themselves to city dwellers looking for exterminators. They are the dog world's "tough guys." Although usually friendly with people, they will not back down from an aggressive incident with other dogs, no matter what their size.

Smooth Fox Terrier

The most popular terrier in the US is the Miniature Schnauzer, ranked 11th in 2003 AKC registrations.

Terrier Group Breeds

15 to 50 pounds:	Manchester Terrier (Standard)	Soft Coated Wheaten Terrier
Australian Terrier	Miniature Bull Terrier	Staffordshire Bull Terrier
Bedlington Terrier	Miniature Schnauzer	Welsh Terrier
Border Terrier	Norfolk Terrier	West Highland White Terrier
Bull Terrier (colored, white)	Norwich Terrier	Wire Fox Terrier
Cairn Terrier	Parson Russell Terrier	**50 to 80 pounds:**
Dandie Dinmont Terrier	Scottish Terrier	Airedale Terrier
Irish Terrier	Sealyham Terrier	American Staffordshire Terrier
Kerry Blue Terrier	Skye Terrier	
Lakeland Terrier	Smooth Fox Terrier	

Miniature Pinscher

Some of the terriers have distinctive double coats, consisting of soft undercoats and wiry jackets that need special grooming. Many are plucked or stripped by hand, which is a time-consuming process that gives them a unique appearance.

The Toy Group

If you are looking for a lot of dog in a small package, a toy breed may be for you. The "toy" part of this breed's name refers to size only. These breeds have such spunk and strong personalities that they often dominate larger dogs, and in some cases, people. Many have descended from larger breeds of terriers or spaniels and still retain those inherent instincts. Others ruled the roost as prized lap dogs and companions to royalty. Despite their small size, they are very vocal defenders of their homes and are ideal pets for those with limited space.

Toy dogs are very popular in the US, and in 2003 the Yorkshire Terrier was ranked 6th in AKC registrations.

Toy Group Breeds

2 to 20 pounds:

Affenpinscher	Havanese	Pomeranian
Brussels Griffon	Italian Greyhound	Pug
Cavalier King Charles Spaniel (Smooth Coat, Long Coat)	Japanese Chin	Shih Tzu
Chihuahua	Maltese	Silky Terrier
Chinese Crested	Manchester Terrier–Toy	Toy Fox Terrier
English Toy Spaniel (Blenheim and Prince Charles, King Charles and Ruby)	Miniature Pinscher	Yorkshire Terrier
	Papillon	
	Pekingese	

Non-Sporting Group Breeds

Under 15 pounds:
Boston Terrier
Löwchen
Poodle—Toy
Schipperke
Tibetan Spaniel

15 to 50 pounds:
American Eskimo Dog
Bichon Frise

Boston Terrier (2 weight classes)
Bulldog
Chinese Shar-Pei
Finnish Spitz
French Bulldog
Keeshond
Lhasa Apso
Poodle—Miniature
Shiba Inu
Tibetan Terrier

50 to 80 pounds:
Chow Chow
Dalmatian
Poodle—Standard

Part 1

The Non-Sporting Group

A diverse collection of breeds, the Non-Sporting Group is made up of those dogs who no longer perform the duties for which they were bred. For example, the Dalmatian is no longer used to accompany horse-drawn carriages, and the Bulldog is no longer used for bullbaiting. They have all found a home in the Non-Sporting Group, which is one of the fastest growing groups in popularity. Included are many popular and well-known breeds that range in size, activity level, coat type, and origin, offering dog owners a choice of breeds to fit every taste.

The Herding Group

Breeds in the Herding Group have been an integral part of every country's use of livestock, and the herding dog still retains many of the physical characteristics and instincts for this work. The

French Bulldog

Herding Group Breeds

15 to 50 pounds:	50 to 80 pounds:
Australian Cattle Dog	Australian Shepherd
Bearded Collie	Belgian Malinois
Border Collie	Belgian Sheepdog
Canaan Dog	Belgian Tervuren
Cardigan Welsh Corgi	Bouvier des Flandres
Pembroke Welsh Corgi	Briard
Polish Lowland Sheepdog	Collie—Rough and Smooth
Puli	German Shepherd Dog
Shetland Sheepdog	Old English Sheepdog

Pembroke Welsh Corgi

herding breeds have been bred to be intelligent, athletic, and diligent and are arguably the most trainable of all breeds, making them naturals for obedience work, agility, and herding trials. Throughout the years, responsible breeders have perpetuated the herding dogs' natural instincts. They have evolved into independent but loyal dogs who are happiest when at work serving their masters. As long as they get enough exercise and mental stimulation, herding dogs can make wonderful, devoted pets who will thrive on (and demand) your companionship.

> The most popular herding breed in the US is the German Shepherd Dog, ranked 4th in 2003 AKC registrations.

The Mixed Breed

Mixed-breed puppies, or "mutts" as they are sometimes affectionately called, can also make great pets. There

Part 1

The Tough Guys

Some dogs will back up their bark with a bite. The following breeds have aggressive tendencies and can exhibit very protective behavior: Akita, Australian Shepherd, Boxer, Doberman Pinscher, German Shepherd Dog, and Rottweiler.

The Heavyweights

Some breeds are more likely to pudge out than others. If you have one of the following breeds, you should pay special attention to keeping your dog fit and trim: Beagle, Cocker Spaniel, Basset Hound, Dachshund, and Labrador Retriever.

are thousands of dogs in shelters all around the country who are just waiting to be adopted. Besides being abundant, mixed breeds, because of their varied backgrounds, may escape many of the genetic problems that purebred dogs face. To ensure that you get the best mixed breed for your family situation, find out as much about the puppy's history, background, and former treatment as possible. It also helps to know what breeds make up the "mix" so that you may better gauge the pup's temperament and needs. Having this information can help predict future problems and allow you to formulate a solution if they should arise.

Although mixed breeds cannot compete in AKC organized events, they can be trained to do anything that a purebred can do, including obedience, agility, flyball, search and rescue, and therapy dog programs. Adopting a mixed breed

Mixed Breed

Part 1

from a shelter will not only provide you with a grateful, lifelong companion, you will have the knowledge that you have saved the life of a special puppy or dog.

Where to Look for Your Puppy

Finding a Breeder

If you have decided that a purebred dog is right for you, you must first find a reputable breeder. This cannot be stressed enough! It is very important that your puppy be purchased from a breeder who has earned a reputation for consistently producing dogs who are physically healthy and mentally sound. Breeders earn that reputation strictly by breeding their dogs selectively. Selective breeding aims to maintain the virtues of a breed and to eliminate genetic weaknesses. A national breed club can assist a prospective dog buyer in finding a responsible breeder of quality puppies.

Selective breeding strives to maintain the virtues of a breed.

Responsible breeders breed for good temperaments.

If you call any of these clubs or log on to their Web sites, you will find that each national breed club will have the name and address or phone number of a member who can refer you to a reputable breeder in your area.

The responsible breeder will breed for good temperaments and will ensure that his or her puppies are properly socialized–the socialization process should not be overlooked. Proper socialization will help produce a mentally stable dog who is able to get along with all kinds of people and other animals. A well-socialized puppy will not show fear, shyness, or aggressiveness.

When searching for a breeder, also consider what kinds of activities you'd like to do with your dog. For example, if you want a Chesapeake Bay Retriever for hunting, try to find a breeder who has bred successful and titled hunting dogs. The breeder should also be able to produce registration papers for the mother and the litter, although these documents may be withheld until some conditions are met, such as spaying or neutering the pup.

With any luck, you will be able to find a reputable breeder in your area who will have at least one of the puppy's parents on the premises. You should see the dam (mother), and although the sire (father) may not be on the premises, you should be able to see a photo of him and find out about his personality. The parents of the puppy should be certified by the Orthopedic Foundation for Animals (OFA) or PennHip™ as being free of hip dysplasia. The Canine Eye Registration Foundation (CERF®) finds animals free of hereditary eye diseases such as cataracts and progressive retinal atrophy in breeds that require such clearance. Good breeders are willing to have you see the dam (and sire) of the litter, as well as inspect the facility where the dogs are raised. The facilities should be clean and the puppies should look well cared for in an area where they can interact with people on a regular basis. These breeders will also be able to discuss the problems that exist in the breed and how they deal with these problems. Knowledgeable breeders are aware of any genetic problems in the breed and take measures to safeguard against them.

Good breeders will allow you to inspect their facilities.

Do not be surprised if a breeder asks lots of questions about you, your family, and the environment in which the puppy will be raised. Good breeders are just as concerned about puppies going to good homes as you are in obtaining a well-adjusted, healthy dog. Breeders will use all of the information you give them to match the right puppy with the right home.

If there are no breeders in your area, you can find legitimate and reliable breeders throughout the country on the national breed club lists. These established breeders can safely ship puppies to different states and even different countries. Always check the references of these breeders and do not hesitate to ask for documentation of their answers.

Most breeders will not allow their puppies to go to their new homes until after they have been given their first vaccinations—usually at about eight weeks of age. Once weaned, your puppy is highly

Puppies should receive their first vaccinations before leaving the breeder.

Healthy puppies appear alert and playful.

susceptible to many infectious diseases that can be transmitted through people. It is best to make sure your puppy is inoculated before leaving the breeder's residence. You should continue the immunization schedule with your veterinarian.

Some people will breed puppies purely for profit or out of ignorance. These are "backyard" breeders, and many of the dogs they breed pass on genetic defects, may not find suitable homes, and end up in shelters. Watch for these signs of a "backyard" breeder:

• Breeds many litters per year
• Knows little about the breed
• Is not involved in the breed club or in dog sports
• Claims not to know about or denies genetic problems in the breed or in the line
• Has no health papers from the veterinarian
• Will not let you see the whole litter, the place they were raised, or either of the puppies' parents
• Does not socialize the dogs
• Asks few or no questions about you or the environment in which the puppy will be raised

Shelters

Most people do not put a lot of thought into acquiring a puppy. They fall in love with a cute face in a pet store window or with a neighborhood bitch's new litter, or they get a dog from the kid selling puppies outside a supermarket. When the dog comes home, he may be too aggressive with the kids, too hard to housetrain, or hyperactive. They may complain that the puppy requires too much time and attention, sheds too much, barks and annoys the neighbors, destroys furniture, or displays a host of other problems. Often, too, someone may find that his or her unspayed female is pregnant and he or she either can't sell or take care of the puppies. Where do all of these dogs go?

Most of these dogs, through no fault of their own, end up in local humane societies and animal shelters throughout the country. Fortunately, these are sites where dedicated people work hard to place dogs in new homes and educate the public about responsible dog ownership. According to the Humane Society of the United States, for every dog who has a home, there are nine other dogs who are homeless or in shelters.

Why do some animals end up in shelters? A study was recently conducted by the National Council on Pet Population whose researchers visited 12 animal shelters for one year and interviewed owners relinquishing their pets. The top ten reasons for giving up pets were as follows: moving, landlord did not allow pet, too many animals in household, cost, personal problems, inadequate facilities, no homes available for littermates, no time to spend with pet, illness, and biting. The study also found that about 47 percent of surrendered dogs were between five months and three years of age. Dogs acquired from friends were relinquished in higher numbers (31.4 percent) than from any other source, and about 95 percent had not received any obedience training.

Many shelter dogs make loyal, loving pets.

Most animal shelters operate as independent agencies, although some fall under the jurisdiction of the city or county and operate with tax dollars. Humane societies are managed by their own board of directors and rely heavily on contributions and volunteers. Both share the common goal of finding homes for as many dogs as possible, and most institutions will require spaying/neutering as a condition of adoption, offering special rates for these procedures.

Although you can visit your local animal shelters or humane societies during their regular hours, many also hold adoption days at pet supply stores and community events. If you find a dog you like, visit a few times and be sure to take the whole family. Ask as many questions as you can about the dog's background. Play with the pup away from the other dogs. If you find a puppy at a shelter, you can perform the puppy aptitude test described later in the book. In turn, the shelter will ask you about your dog-owning history and have you fill out a questionnaire that describes your home, work, and living situation and asks you to give veterinary references. This will help them make sure that the right dog goes to the right person.

Once you've been approved, you will pay an adoption fee. Some shelters will include vaccinations and training programs at a discounted rate. Although the actual adoption process will vary, people who adopt from shelters all go home with the same thing—a new best friend.

Purebred rescue groups can help you find the perfect puppy.

Rescue

Most national breed clubs sponsor rescue groups that help place dogs into new homes. Although they mostly deal with adult dogs, a purebred rescue group can be a good way to find a puppy. Most of them work in conjunction with animal shelters, which alert the rescue organization if a purebred dog is brought in. The volunteers will provide foster homes for the dogs, assess their health and temperament, screen them for training and social skills, and care for the dogs until they find new homes.

As mentioned before, most of the dogs fostered in rescue programs are adults, but you can call and ask to be put on the waiting list for a puppy. You can get in touch with a breed rescue in your area by calling the local humane society or the AKC. Both maintain a list of national breed rescue coordinators.

Selecting a Healthy Puppy–From Head to Toe

When looking for a new puppy, begin by examining the whole litter. In general, are they kept clean and sanitary? The puppies should be kept in an environment that is conducive to socialization–they should be around people and handled regularly. Do the puppies look active and alert or do they look sluggish? Is the mother healthy looking and displaying a friendly temperament? Do the puppies seem fearful of people or are they inquisitive and curious? Just watching the litter and how they interact can tell you a lot about their general health as well as about the individual personalities of each puppy.

Puppies should be around people and handled regularly from an early age.

How to Spot a Healthy Puppy:

✓ Clear, bright eyes

✓ Pink, odor-free ears

✓ Clean, shiny coat

✓ Sweet "puppy" breath

✓ Clean anal region

✓ Alert, curious attitude

Don't Do It!

Although it may be tempting to pick a sick puppy and take him home because you feel sorry for him, this is never a good idea. The heartache you will experience (and the veterinary bills) will not be worth it.

Next, pick up and give each puppy a thorough once-over. A puppy should feel solid, with firm, well-developed muscles. A healthy puppy will **not** feel bony, bloated, or obese. Each puppy should have a clean and shiny coat, with no signs of irritation or sores on the skin. The eyes should be bright, clear, and free from discharge. Their ears should be pink inside and smell clean— a bad odor or waxy discharge could indicate ear mites. Their gums should be pink and their breath should smell sweet—not minty-fresh, but not sour or foul. Their anal region should be clean and dry, with no signs of diarrhea, discharge, or irritation. Obvious coughing, sneezing, or wheezing are clear indications of illness, as are runny eyes and noses.

Once you have determined that the puppies are healthy and you feel comfortable with the surroundings, you can begin to narrow down the choices in order to find the puppy who will best fit your needs, lifestyle, and personality.

Temperament Testing

Whether you have decided on a purebred or a mixed-breed puppy, the dog's temperament will be an important part of deciding which puppy you should take home. You will want to pick the puppy with a personality that will fit with yours and the rest of your

Select a puppy whose temperament fits best with Yours.

family's. You will also want to choose the puppy who will be able to do the things you want, whether it is to compete in events like obedience or agility, work as an assistance or therapy dog, or just take part in family activities. Not only are the dog's physical abilities important in this respect, but the puppy's temperament and trainability are large factors in picking the puppy you will be happy with (and that will be happy with you) for the rest of your lives together.

You can test a puppy's personality by using a puppy aptitude test. The Puppy Aptitude Test, or PAT, developed by Wendy Volhard as published in the AKC *Gazette,* indicates which pup in a litter would have the most aptitude for a desired task or purpose. The sequence of the test is the same for all puppies and is designed to alternate a slightly stressful element with a neutral or pleasant one. Ideally, these conditions would be set before testing takes place.

Puppies should be tested in the 7th week of life, preferably on the 49th day. Before the 7th week, the puppy's neurological connections are not developed, and after the 8th week, the puppy will be in a fear imprint stage and is more easily frightened.

Social Attraction

Test	Purpose	Score
With the puppy in the ideal testing area, the tester should coax the puppy to come by kneeling down and gently clapping. The tester should stand a few feet away and coax the puppy in the opposite direction of where the pup entered the area.	This will gauge the puppy's degree of social attraction, confidence, or dependence.	1 Came readily, tail up, jumped, bit at hands 2 Came readily, tail up, pawed, licked at hands 3 Came readily, tail up 4 Came readily, tail down 5 Came hesitantly, tail down 6 Did not come at all

Following

Test	Purpose	Score
The tester should stand up and walk away from the puppy in a normal manner, making sure the puppy sees him or her walk away.	This will gauge the puppy's degree of following attraction. Not following the tester indicates independence.	1 Followed readily, tail up, got underfoot, bit at feet 2 Followed readily, tail up, bit at feet 3 Followed readily, tail up 4 Followed hesitantly, tail down 5 Did not follow or went away 6 Went in different direction

Restraint

Test	Purpose	Score
The tester should crouch down and gently roll the pup over and hold the dog on his back with one hand for a full 30 seconds.	This will test whether the puppy has dominant or submissive tendencies and to what degree. It will also test how the puppy handles the stress of being socially or physically dominated.	1 Struggled fiercely, flailed, bit 2 Struggled fiercely, flailed 3 Struggled, settled with some eye contact 4 Struggled then settled 5 No struggle 6 No struggle, straining to avoid eye contact

Social Dominance

Test	Purpose	Score
The tester should let the pup stand and while crouching beside him, should gently stroke the pup from head to tail. Continue stroking the puppy until a recognizable behavior is established.	This will test the puppy's acceptance of social dominance.	1 Jumped, pawed, bit, growled 2 Jumped, pawed 3 Cuddled up to tester and tried to lick face 4 Squirmed, licked at hands 5 Rolled over, licked at hands 6 Went away and stayed away

Elevation Dominance

Test	Purpose	Score
The tester should stand over the puppy and cradle him under the belly, fingers interlaced and palms up, and elevate the pup just off the ground for 30 seconds.	This will determine how the pup accepts dominance while in the position of having no control.	1 Struggled fiercely, bit, and growled 2 Struggled fiercely 3 No struggle, relaxed 4 Struggled, settled, and licked 5 No struggle, licked at hands 6 No struggle, froze

Part 1

Part 1

Retrieving

Test	Purpose	Score
The tester should crouch down beside the puppy and attract the pup's attention with a crumpled ball of paper. When the dog is showing interest and watching the tester, he or she should toss the object 4 to 6 feet in front of the pup.	This tests the puppy's willingness to work with a human. There has been a high correlation between a puppy's ability to retrieve and his subsequent success as a guide dog, obedience dog, and field trial dog.	1 Chased and picked up object and ran away 2 Chased object, stood over it, but did not return it 3 Chased object and returned object to tester 4 Chased object and returned to tester without object 5 Started to chase object but lost interest 6 Did not chase object

Touch Sensitivity

Test	Purpose	Score
While slowly counting to ten, the tester should take the puppy's front foot and press the webbing between finger and thumb lightly and then more firmly until he gets a response. Stop as soon as the puppy pulls away or shows discomfort.	This test gauges the puppy's degree of sensitivity to touch.	1 Eight to ten counts before puppy responded 2 Six to seven counts before puppy responded 3 Five to six counts before puppy responded 4 Two to four counts before puppy responded 5 One to two counts before puppy responded 6 Cringed from touch entirely

Sound Sensitivity

Test	Purpose	Score
With the pup in the center of the testing area, the tester should make a sharp noise a few feet away from the puppy. A large metal spoon struck sharply on a metal pan works well.	This tests the puppy's degree of sensitivity to sound and can also be a rudimentary test for deafness.	1 Listened, located sound, walked toward it, and barked 2 Listened, located sound, and barked 3 Listened, located sound, showed curiosity, and walked toward sound 4 Listened, located sound 5 Cringed, backed off, and hid 6 Ignored sound and showed no curiosity

Sight Sensitivity

Test	Purpose	Score
The tester should place the pup in the middle of the testing area. He or she should then tie a string around a large towel and jerk it across the floor a few feet away from the puppy.	This measures the pup's degree of intelligent response to a strange object.	1 Looked at object, attacked, and bit 2 Looked at object, barked, and put his tail up 3 Looked curiously and attempted to investigate 4 Looked, barked, and tucked his tail under 5 Had no response 6 Ran away and hid

Puppies should be tested individually, away from their dam and littermates. They should be taken to an area that is unfamiliar to them and relatively free of distractions. They should also be tested before they have eaten, while they are awake and lively, and not on a day when they have been wormed or vaccinated. The puppy you select should be tested by someone other than the litter owner in order to reduce the chance of either human error or the puppy being influenced by someone familiar.

The prospective puppy owner should be able to see and observe the temperament and behavior of both the dam and littermates. The puppy will often display the characteristics and personality of the parents.

How to Interpret the Scores:
Mostly 1's:
This puppy is extremely dominant and has aggressive tendencies. This type of dog is quick to bite and generally not considered good with children and the elderly. When combined with a 1 or 2 in touch sensitivity, this indicates that the puppy will be difficult to train. This puppy is not a good choice for an inexperienced dog handler and will need a competent trainer to establish leadership.

Mostly 2's:
This puppy has a dominant personality and can be provoked to bite. He responds well to firm, consistent, and fair handling in an adult household and is likely to be a loyal pet once respect for the owner is established. This puppy often has a bouncy, outgoing temperament and may be too active for the elderly and too dominant for a household with small children.

Mostly 3's:
This puppy will accept a human leader easily and will adapt well to new situations. Although active, this kind of dog will generally be good with children and the elderly, will have potential to be a good obedience dog, and will usually display a common-sense approach to life.

Mostly 4's:

This puppy has a submissive personality. He will adapt to most households and may be slightly less outgoing but will get along with children and accept training well.

Mostly 5's:

With an extremely submissive personality, this puppy will need special handling to build confidence and come out of his shell. A pup with this personality does not adapt well to change or confusion and needs a regular schedule and structured environment. He can usually be considered safe around children and will bite only when severely stressed. This puppy is not a good choice for beginners because he frightens easily and takes a long time to get used to new experiences.

Mostly 6's:

This puppy is independent, may not be affectionate, and may dislike petting or cuddling. Whether a pet or a working dog, it will be difficult to establish a relationship with this dog whose personality is not recommended for a household with children who may force attention on him. When this puppy's score is combined with a lot of 1's, especially in the restraint tests, he may be likely to bite under stress. When combined with a lot of 5's, this pup may be likely to hide from people or freeze when approached by a stranger.

If there is no clear pattern to the test scores, your puppy may not be feeling well or may have just eaten or been wormed. Wait two days and retest. If the test still shows a lot of variation, the puppy is probably unpredictable and is unlikely to be a good pet or obedience dog.

Prospective puppy owners should examine the temperaments of the dam and littermates.

In Conclusion

By now, you have done your research, decided on and found the type of puppy you want, confirmed the pup's health, and tested temperament. You have done all you can to ensure that you get off to a good start, even before you bring your new puppy home. Well, the big day is here! It's time to prepare to get your perfect puppy and get going!

Getting Prepared

There are a few things you should do before a puppy steps into your home. To ensure that you begin on the right foot, remember that puppies are just like babies. You wouldn't bring home a new baby before you had a crib, diapers, clothes, and all of the other equipment you need to keep a child safe and comfortable. The same holds true for your new canine addition.

Veterinary Care

The first thing you should do is find a good veterinarian in your area. Within 72 hours of arriving home, your pup should visit the vet for a

Your new puppy should immediately visit the veterinarian for a complete exam.

Leaving the Nest

The best time for a puppy to leave his mother is generally about nine weeks of age. Before the seventh week, puppies are not mentally mature or independent enough to leave the security of their mom and littermates. At eight weeks, puppies go through a fear-imprinting period. Any experience that frightens a puppy at this stage, such as an unpleasant car ride or rough play with children, may remain with him for a long time. If you do bring home a puppy in the eighth week, make sure that you provide him with many positive experiences.

complete exam and to continue a vaccination schedule. Also, you never know when an emergency may arise, so select your veterinarian before bringing your puppy home.

When searching for a vet, try several sources. You can ask your local humane society or animal shelter, your dog-owning friends, or the puppy's breeder for recommendations. Once you have the names of a few veterinarians, you should visit each one. Check out the facilities and meet the doctor and staff. Inspect the office and make sure it is clean, well lit, and sufficiently supervised. Make sure the veterinarian is familiar with your breed. Ask about hospital hours, emergency policies, payment policies, and the clinic's specialties. Once you are comfortable with your choice, you can make an appointment for your puppy.

License to Own

Make sure your pooch is legal. Call your town hall or animal control office and ask when your dog requires a license, which is usually at about six months of age. Many towns will also require proof that your dog has been vaccinated for rabies. Find out what other local laws apply to your dog. Most towns have leash laws and clean-up laws, with stiff fines for people who don't follow them. You should also get your dog an ID tag that states the dog's name and your name, address, and phone number. This will be very helpful in case the dog gets lost.

Preparing for Your Puppy

There are certain things that your puppy will need immediately, so it is best to purchase these items

Call your town hall to find out what local laws apply to your dog.

before he comes home. The better prepared you are for the puppy's arrival, the smoother the transition will be for everyone.

What's in a Name?

Naming a new puppy may be one of the most enjoyable aspects of getting one. Some people like to pick a name that indicates the dog's origins or appearance, (I know an Australian Shepherd named Sydney and an Irish Setter named Copper) or their other interests. (I know a Star Trek fan who has a Beagle named Spock and an English professor who has two chocolate Labs named Romeo and Juliet.) Some people choose "people" names like Fred, Chester, Rosie, or Jake. Names can come from anywhere: cities, television shows, literature, movies–all it takes is a little imagination to pick a name that perfectly fits your puppy's personality.

You should try to make the puppy's name short, one or two syllables, and you shouldn't pick a name that may sound too close to a command, like Six or Downy, which may confuse your dog during training. Most of all, you should never say your puppy's name in a loud or threatening tone or call the dog to you for a scolding. You want your puppy to jump with joy and excitement when hearing his name, no matter what it is!

Food and Water Bowls

When it comes to food and water bowls for your puppy, there is one guarantee–chewable bowls

> *Things You Need for the Puppy's Arrival:*
> - Food & water bowls
> - Puppy food
> - Collar & leash
> - Crate
> - Baby gates
> - Grooming tools
> - Toys
> - ID tag

The best bowls to buy are made of stainless steel or ceramic.

At least part of your yard should be enclosed for your puppy's safety.

Accustom your puppy to his collar before you introduce him to the leash.

will be chewed and breakable bowls will be broken. Nothing could be more fun for your puppy than spilling food and water all over your kitchen floor. The best bowls to buy are stainless steel or ceramic bowls that are wide on the bottom and heavy so that they won't spill, saving you hours of cleanup and lots of money in the long run.

Puppy Food

Speak to the breeder and find out what the puppy has been eating. It is wise to purchase the same food for at least the first few weeks. Switching food suddenly can cause stomach upset and diarrhea. If you wish to change the brand of food, you can do so gradually over an extended period of time. The feeding chapter will give you more details on the best nutrition for your puppy.

Collar and Leash

One of the first things your puppy should learn is to wear a collar and walk on a leash. You should buy an adjustable, soft, nylon buckle collar and a 4- to 6-foot leash. You may need more advanced training collars and leashes as the puppy matures, but these two pieces of equipment will be fine to start with.

ID Tag

Every dog should have an identification tag attached to his collar that has his owner's name, address, and phone number engraved on it. This information will make it easier for someone to contact you in the event that your puppy should become lost.

There are several methods of dog identification available today. The first is tattooing. The dog's inner thigh or ear flap is permanently tattooed with numbers that are then registered with one of the national registries. This makes it possible for the registry companies to contact you if your dog turns up at a shelter. Also, research laboratories will not take dogs who have been tattooed.

Second is the microchip, a small computer chip that can be placed under your dog's skin. If a dog is picked up by animal control, the chip can be scanned and the dog's owner can be identified. There are a few microchip registry companies in practice, and they do share information with each other.

A microchip can help identify your dog should he become lost.

Crates

A crate serves as a dog's own room. It is a very important purchase because it has so many uses: it is a great housetraining tool, a safe way for your dog to travel, and a comfortable bed where the pup can sleep, retreat, and relax. Using a crate is the easiest and fastest way to housetrain and is great when you can't supervise your dog.

There are two types of crates: plastic or fiberglass airline-type crates with enclosed sides and open metal wire crates. The plastic crates are good to use for traveling, especially by air, and some dogs feel more secure in an enclosed space. The wire crates provide

The crate is an effective housetraining tool.

If the Toy Fits . . .

Make sure that you buy the right size toys for your pup. Most packages will indicate the size dog for which the toy is made. Make sure you monitor the dog's chewing, and when the toy gets too small or pieces start to break off, take the toy away and dispose of it. This will prevent the pup from choking on small pieces or swallowing larger pieces that could get lodged in the stomach or intestine.

more ventilation in hotter weather and more room to move around. Consider how you will be using the crate and pick the best one to fit your needs.

A crate is an expensive item, so buy one that will fit your dog's adult size. An adult dog should be able to stand up, turn around, and stretch out in the crate. However, you don't want your little puppy to have too much room either. One suggestion is to block the back of the crate with a piece of plywood when the pup is small and make the space bigger as he matures.

Baby Gates

Baby gates are very useful for keeping your puppy confined in a safe place. You can also block the puppy's access to other rooms and stairs, or restrict access to anything that may be unsafe.

Grooming Tools

No matter what breed, your puppy will need to be groomed on a regular basis. You will need to purchase some basic grooming tools such as a comb and brush (the type of comb and brush you buy will depend on the kind of coat your puppy has), nail clippers, and a good dog shampoo and conditioner.

Toys

All puppies need to chew as part of their physical and mental development. At about four weeks of age, your puppy's deciduous (baby) teeth will come in. Pups will need to strengthen their jaw muscles and make room for

A brush is a necessary grooming tool.

future adult teeth. Chewing helps them to explore the world. Good, safe toys will entertain and give your puppy something to chew on other than your shoes or furniture. Not only are toys healthy, they are a fun way of keeping your puppy occupied. Playing together will help to strengthen the bond between the two of you.

Settling In

Once you have all the basic equipment ready for your puppy, you should set up a tentative schedule with your family. Figure out who can be with the pup and when, because any dog needs constant supervision for the first few days. The worst thing you can do is to leave a new puppy alone. He will be unsure of the environment. Your puppy will be scared and lonely, and his first impressions will last a long time.

Think about where the puppy will eat, sleep, and be taken to eliminate. It is also a good time to take a look at your existing environment and see if your home is safe enough for the pup.

Laundry Hints

More than one puppy has climbed into the washing machine for a quick nap and been caught in the rinse cycle instead. If the washing machine door is open, be sure to check inside the machine before you close the door and switch the machine on.

Puppy-Proofing Your Home

Your new puppy will be very curious about his new surroundings, and with typical puppy energy, will want to investigate everything. The trick is to make the dangerous things unavailable by puppy-proofing your home. The best way to do this is to get down on the pup's level and take a look around. What can he get into? What can he jump up on? What can your pup open or chew on? Don't ever assume that the puppy won't touch something; if pups can get

Puppy-proof any areas to which your puppy has access.

Part 1

Carefully supervise your dog when playing outdoors.

Plants That Are Poisonous to Your Dog:

Amaryllis bulbs, andromeda, apple seeds, arrowgrass, avocado, azalea, bittersweet, boxwood, buttercup, caladium, castor bean, cherry pits, chokecherry, climbing lily, crown of thorns, daffodil bulb, daphne, delphinium, dieffenbachia, dumb cane, elderberry, elephant ear, English ivy, foxglove, hemlock, holly, hyancinth, hydrangea, iris, japanese yew, jasmine berries, Jerusalem cherry, jimson weed, laburnum, larkspur, laurel, marigold, marijuana, mistletoe berries, monkshood, mushrooms, narcissus, nightshade, oleander, peach, philodendren, poison ivy, privet, rhododendron, rhubarb, snow on the mountain, stinging nettle, toadstool, tobacco, tulip bulb, walnut, wisteria, yew.

into trouble, they will. There are many potential dangers in the home, so you must think about these in advance and make sure your new puppy is protected from them.

Electrical Wires

Be sure that all electrical wires are hidden from view and not plugged in when not in use. Even wires from appliances that are turned off, such as lamps or television sets, can be dangerous. To be safe, unplug anything electric if it is not currently being used.

Open Doors

Puppies can easily get underfoot or sneak up on you. A door may seem like a pretty harmless object, but if it is slammed shut, either by a draft or by accident, it could easily kill or injure a puppy. During warm weather, windows or doors are left open and people are more likely to run in and out. Know where your puppy is at all times and make sure that everyone in your household knows to keep doors securely shut.

Balconies

If you live in an apartment building or house that has a balcony, you must make sure that your puppy cannot fall. Check the railings on your patio, balcony, or deck, and if the space between them is too large, you can use inexpensive chicken wire or baby gates to form a temporary screen.

Ponds and Pools

Lots of dogs like the water and love to swim, but your puppy must be taught to get in and out of your pool safely. Many dogs will jump headfirst into a swimming pool and have no idea how to get out. There will be plenty of time to introduce swimming as the puppy strengthens and matures. Never leave your puppy unsupervised near water, and keep pools or ponds covered if you can't be there. It only takes a few minutes for a puppy to drown while your back is turned.

The Kitchen

Your puppy will probably spend a lot of time in the kitchen. It is usually where most of the family congregates, and is probably the most convenient place to feed your pup and to clean up any messes he may make.

However, the kitchen can be filled with lots of dangers. Make sure the cupboards are securely fastened at all times or buy locks. Place all cleaning supplies, detergents, and solvents in locked cupboards, or place them well out of your dog's reach.

It is also a good idea to keep the garbage hidden or the lid tightly closed. There is nothing more tempting to dogs than the aroma of garbage, and nothing could be worse for them. The garbage

Keep all kitchen items out of reach of your puppy.

Food left on the counter may provide a tempting target for your dog.

may hold spoiled food or items like chicken bones or chocolate, which can make them seriously ill.

Be careful of what you are leaving on tables or counters as well. Everyone has heard the story of the dog who jumped up and ate the Thanksgiving turkey, the Easter candy, or the birthday cake left on the counter. It may not seem as if your tiny pup can get up that high, but puppies are ingenious at getting into things they shouldn't—especially if it involves food.

Also, be careful when cooking. Rambunctious puppies can jump up and knock over pots and pans, causing serious injury. It is a good idea to confine your puppy to a crate before you cook a meal.

Bathrooms

When puppy-proofing your home, bathrooms should be treated like kitchens. Securely fasten or lock all cupboards and medicine chests. Keep all cleansers and detergents out of reach. Place all soaps and shampoos in a shower caddy so that your puppy can't get to them. Be especially careful of decorative soaps—if they smell good, your puppy will try to eat them.

A baby gate will help prevent your puppy from getting into trouble.

Keep the toilet seat cover down at all times. Curious puppies have been known to climb up and fall in. The best advice is to keep doors shut to all rooms where the puppy should not have access unless you can supervise him. Puppies can't get *into* trouble if they can't get *to* the trouble in the first place.

The Yard

The yard should be a fun place for your puppy to hang out and play, but you must take the necessary precautions to make it as safe as possible. First, you must make sure that the yard is securely fenced and that there is no way for your puppy to escape. Check that all fences are strong and that there are no holes in the wire or near the ground. Make sure that there is a secure lock on the gate and that everyone in your family knows to fasten it when they come in or out of the yard. Pick up any toys, lawn furniture, or gardening tools that you don't want your puppy to play with. Whatever puppies can chew, they will.

Make your yard as safe as possible for your curious puppy.

If there is a particular area of your yard where you do not want your puppy to go, such as the garden, fence that area off. Be careful what pesticides or fertilizers you use on your lawn. Do not let the puppy into a yard where chemicals have been used. Make sure you store any chemicals where your puppy can't get to them.

Remember that some plants are poisonous to puppies. Check your yard to make sure these plants are not present. If your dog eats something he shouldn't, you can call the National Animal Poison Control Center (NAPCC). They have a staff of over 40 licensed vets and board certified toxicologists. They can be reached 24 hours a day. Call 1-800-548-2423.

If your fence is not secure or you don't want to give your puppy free reign of the yard, you may want to consider building a dog run. It should be about 20 feet long and about 6 feet wide and should have some shade. You should also provide water and a clean, comfortable place for the pup to lie down.

Part 1

A Child's Ten Commandments for Puppy Care

- Thou shall treat all animals as you would like to be treated—gently, kindly, and respectfully.
- Thou shall not lift the puppy unless you have been taught to do it properly and an adult is nearby.
- Thou shall not disturb the puppy while he is eating or sleeping.
- Thou shall not share your snacks.
- Thou shall keep your toys and the puppy's toys separate.

- Thou shall not tease.
- Thou shall not approach any strange dog.
- Thou shall help the puppy follow the rules of the house and not allow him to disobey the rules.
- Thou shall honor your puppy as a living thing and take responsibility for his care and well-being.
- Thou shall enjoy the years of love and friendship your puppy gives you—and remember to give it back.

The Garage

If you have a garage or tool shed, make sure that this is puppy-proofed too. Many people keep potential hazards to their pets in garages, such as antifreeze, motor oil, gasoline, fertilizer, insecticides, paint, and paint removers, among other things. People also keep tools in the garage, such as saws, hammers, nails, and knives, which obviously can be very dangerous as well. Put these things out of your puppy's reach or keep them safely locked up.

Preparing Your Family

A Kid's Best Friend

When you are ready to bring your puppy home, it is very likely that the most excited members of your family will be your children. However, in their enthusiasm, children can get carried away and

Dog ownership teaches children responsibility.

unintentionally hurt or frighten a small puppy. To make sure that the transition goes as smoothly as possible, you must set some ground rules before the puppy arrives.

Children should be taught from the outset that a puppy is not a plaything to be dragged around, and they should be scolded promptly if they disobey. Toddlers and small children should never be left unsupervised with puppies. They must be taught to respect animals and to be gentle with them. If the puppy is frightened by children, the feeling might continue as the pup matures. Also, the puppy may nip or scratch in fear, which could harm or scare your children. *Mutual regard for one another must be taught from the outset.* Teach children that your puppy is a living thing with feelings and can be hurt. Make sure that the pup is given a break and allowed to have quiet time away from excited "siblings."

Children also must be shown how to lift a puppy safely. Teach your kids to place the right hand under the pup's chest, then use the left hand to hold the pup's neck. Now they can lift the dog and bring him close to their chest, supporting the rump with their left hand. Never lift a pup by the ears or by the scruff of the neck.

Remember that puppies are very much like children. Most likely, the puppy will find your child to be the most exciting person in the house. But puppies, much like children, need limits. They also need to rest often and be allowed to relax. If you teach your puppy and your child to be gentle and respect each other, there is no doubt that they will soon become the best of friends.

Puppy Comes Home

You've been shopping, your house is ready, your kids are ready, you are ready–it's time to pick up your puppy. If possible, you should arrange to take a few days off. If this is not possible, pick up the puppy on a Friday in order to spend as much time as you can helping him get adjusted. A morning pickup is best, because that will give the puppy all day to explore his new surroundings.

If the breeder is only a short distance away, you should bring a small cardboard box or a crate for the pup, a blanket, and towels to clean up any messes. Puppies tend to get carsick,

A morning pickup will give your puppy all day to adjust to his new home.

Bring a collar and leash when you pick up the puppy.

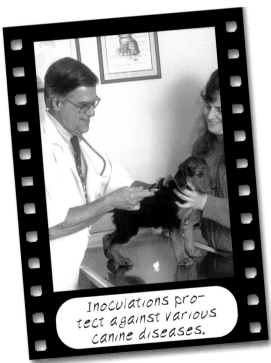

Inoculations protect against various canine diseases.

especially if it is their first ride, and they may throw up or urinate. Keeping the car well ventilated may help. Also, be sure to tell the breeder what time you will be picking the puppy up, so the dog's meals can be planned accordingly.

If it is a longer ride, make frequent stops. Bring along a collar and leash so you can take the dog out to exercise and potty. Do not let your new pup near other dogs or where other dogs have been until all vaccinations have been completed.

Leaving the Breeder

Before you leave the breeder, there are certain documents you should receive that will include important information about your puppy.

Inoculation Record

The breeder should have initiated the necessary inoculations by the time the puppies are eight weeks of age, so your puppy should have been given his first shots before leaving the breeder. These inoculations protect the puppies against hepatitis, leptospirosis, distemper, and canine parvovirus. In most cases, rabies inoculations are not given until a puppy is four months of age or older. (A suggested schedule for inoculations is given in the health chapter.)

Inoculations are usually given as a series, and it is very important that your puppy receives the full set in order for them to be effective. Be sure that the breeder

> ### Quarantine!
> Dogs can transmit diseases to other dogs, and people can carry bacteria on their hands or clothes that can be passed to the puppy. Until vaccinations have been completed, it is best to limit visitors, both canine and human.

provides you with the puppy's record and the name of his veterinarian before you bring your pup home. This way, you can show the information to the veterinarian you have chosen, who will then be able to continue with an appropriate inoculation schedule.

Pedigrees show a puppy's ancestors back to at least the third generation.

Pedigree

If your puppy is a purebred, the breeder must supply you with a pedigree. This shows your puppy's ancestors back to at least the third generation. The pedigree can be helpful in determining if your puppy's relatives have titles in conformation, agility, obedience, or field trials, which can indicate the trainability and work ethic of the pup's parents, grandparents, etc.

Registration Certificate

A national kennel club registry issues a registration certificate when the puppy's parents and ancestors are also registered. When ownership of a puppy is transferred from the breeder's name to your name, the

> ### It's All in the Papers
> All purebred dogs have a pedigree. The pedigree does not imply that a dog is show quality but is simply a chronological list of ancestors. Also, registration papers only guarantee that a dog is registerable, nothing else. Neither paper is a guarantee of the health nor quality of your dog.

A breeder's diet sheet details what food your puppy has been eating.

transfer is recorded on this document. Once this is mailed to the kennel club, it is permanently recorded in their files.

Diet Sheet

Most breeders will give the new owner a written record detailing the amount and kind of food a puppy has been eating. Follow these recommendations exactly, at least for the first few weeks after the puppy comes to live with you. The instructions should indicate the number of times a day your puppy has been fed, as well as the kind of vitamin supplementation, if any. If you follow the breeder's instructions, it will greatly reduce the chance of your puppy suffering from an upset stomach and diarrhea.

The breeder's diet sheet should project the increases and changes that will be necessary as your puppy grows. If the breeder does not provide you with this information, ask your veterinarian for suggestions. If and when you decide to change the type or brand of dog food you are giving your puppy, do so gradually, mixing the old food with the new until the substitution is completed.

Health Guarantee

Reputable breeders will be more than willing to supply a written agreement that the puppy you take home must be able to pass a veterinarian's examination. Furthermore, they should offer a guarantee against the development of any hereditary problems. As mentioned

Many breeders will provide a health guarantee with their puppies.

Arrange an appointment with your vet as soon as possible.

The initial vet exam is crucial to your pup's future health and well-being.

before, you should arrange an appointment with a veterinarian within a few days of bringing the pup home. Most breeders are as anxious as you to ensure that the puppy is happy and comfortable in your home. Many will give you a breed book that has instructions on basic care and training. Breeders want to follow the progress of their dogs, so they will be willing to answer any questions you may have.

If you are taking your puppy home from a humane society or animal shelter, you will not get all the paperwork that you will get from a breeder. Depending on the organization, you will probably leave with an inoculation record and a feeding schedule that includes the brand of dog food used at the shelter. You may get information on training classes available in the area. If you have any questions about the dog's health or care, ask. Most shelter volunteers are eager to help you make your puppy as comfortable as possible.

First Night

Trainer Alexandra Allred has a tip to help your puppy adjust to his new home: Allow the pup to sleep with a few articles of your clothing, preferably something you have worn that smells like you. This way, your puppy will become adjusted to your scent and will feel more comfortable in this new environment.

A warm blanket and soft toys will make the crate more welcoming.

Introducing your puppy to other dogs is part of the socialization process.

The First Few Days

The first few nights that a puppy spends away from mom and littermates may be frightening. Being in a strange environment with new sounds and new people will probably make your pup feel scared, insecure, and lonely. It is very important to try to make your new addition as comfortable as possible, which is why it's a good idea to take some time off to help with the transition. Try to refrain from overwhelming the dog with new people or things, and allow the pup to adjust to and explore your home at his own pace. Introduce the schedule that you have set up to establish a routine as soon as possible.

Your puppy may whimper or cry at night. For the first few nights, you should provide as much comfort as possible by offering a warm blanket, soft toys, and a dim nightlight. However, don't let the pup do anything now that you are not planning to allow in the future. For example, if you do not want your dog to sleep on the bed or the furniture, don't allow him to do so now. However, you might bring your pup's bed or crate into your room to be near you. As the days pass, the youngster will become used to the new environment and should become more comfortable.

The worst thing you can do is yell at or scold a scared puppy for making noise or crying. This will only make matters worse and teach your puppy to fear you instead of trust you. Remember that each puppy is an individual and will need different levels of attention. It is important to find a balance between coddling and comforting.

Other Pets

If you have other pets in your home, you will need to introduce the puppy to them carefully, depending on what kind of pets you already have. Puppies will usually have no problems meeting other animals, but the other animal whose turf is being invaded may have a problem with the puppy. The best thing to do is to keep them separated until they are used to each other. Most older dogs will accept a

Other household pets should be carefully introduced to your puppy.

puppy without a fuss and will quickly teach the puppy who is the boss. Cats will not have a lot of patience with a rambunctious, playful puppy, and he may get a scratch for stepping over the line. Also, small animals like rabbits or hamsters should be kept out of the puppy's reach. If you make introductions slowly and carefully and supervise the animals when they are together, they will eventually learn to co-exist and may even become good friends in the process.

Now your puppy is safe and sound and may even be starting to like his new home. However, your journey is just beginning. Remember that you are responsible for all of the aspects of this youngster's care–mental and physical. One important way to start on the road to a good relationship is to familiarize yourself with your puppy's thought processes and development. The next chapter should give you some insight into your pup's mind and help you to form a strong bond that will last throughout your life together.

Understanding Your Puppy

Pack Mentality

Most researchers agree that today's pet dogs descended from wolves. Eventually, we discovered that wild canids could be domesticated and bred to perform certain tasks. Although the call of the wild has been selectively bred out of these wolves for centuries, dogs have natural instincts that are inherent. No matter what kind of environment they live in today, dogs will always have a bit of the wolf in them.

Wolves are social creatures that live in an extended family pack, which consists of a

Like wolves, dogs are pack animals.

The term "alpha" refers to the dominant male and female in a pack.

How Old Is Your Dog?

According to Bonnie Wilcox, D.V.M. and Chris Walkowicz in their book *Old Dogs, Old Friends*, dogs age most quickly during their first year of life and then approximately four years for every one human year.

Dog Age	=	Human Years
6 months		10 years
8 months		13 years
10 months		14 years
12 months		15 years
18 months		20 years
2 years		24 years
4 years		32 years
6 years		40 years
8 years		48 years
10 years		56 years
12 years		64 years
14 years		72 years
16 years		80 years

dominant (alpha) male and a dominant (alpha) female. These alphas breed together. In the pack, there will also be subordinate males, females, juveniles, and puppies–a usually harmonious group that hunts together, shares food, plays together, defends its territory against intruders, and cares for each other. Occasionally, the pack order will be disrupted when change occurs. If one of the leaders becomes injured, if an adult leaves the pack, or if a subordinate adult or juvenile tries to step up in the order and assume dominance, there may be discord and infighting until the positions are settled again.

Many feel that the reason domesticated dogs adapted so well to humans is because we also live in groups. We call them families instead of packs, but they are still social and follow a similar hierarchy. When puppies join a household, they are entering into a new pack. They will naturally look to find the pack leader–the alpha–to teach the rules of this new group.

It can be very confusing for a pup because our families are much more disorderly than the average wolf pack. We can be very inconsistent when enforcing our social and behavior rules; sometimes behaviors are accepted one day and punished the next. Human communication makes no sense to a dog because the tone of our voice can mean one thing, while our body language says something else. If not given a leader and rules to follow, your puppy will assume the alpha role and make up his own rules. Knowing these principles can help you better relate to and train your puppy. If you study the stages of a puppy's development, learn to read his body language, and attempt to see the world through your canine's eyes, you can discover a lot about dog behavior.

How Puppies Develop

Most development occurs during the first year of life, which is why it is so important to get on the right track from birth. If not provided with the proper socialization, nutrition, health care, training, and affection during this first year, dogs will have a hard time fitting in with their human family–or society in general.

The Newborn Puppy

For the first three weeks of a puppy's life, the

In a family situation, you should assume the alpha role.

Leader of the Pack

Between 8 and 12 weeks of age, pack instincts are developing. Your pup is beginning to understand who belongs to the pack and who does not. He is also trying to find a place in the pack order. You can show your dog his position in the family in several different ways. One of the easiest ways to show a pup that he is submissive to you is to lay him down, roll him over, and give him a tummy rub. Have all members of the family try this, including your kids. The exercise may seem very simple, but by baring his tummy he is assuming a submissive position. Earlier in the pup's life, his mother imposed discipline by growling or barking, and she would roll the pup over with his tummy bared to her. When you have your dog roll over for a tummy rub, you are teaching him that you are the boss, but you are doing it in a very gentle, loving way.

only being of any significance is his mother. She is the source of food, warmth, and security. Like a newborn baby, the newborn puppy doesn't do much of anything except eat, sleep, and eliminate.

At four weeks of age, the puppy's littermates are becoming more important. Brothers and sisters provide warmth and security when mother leaves the nest. The puppies are becoming slightly more aware of their environment, and curiosity is beginning to develop. Although their mother is still taking care of their basic needs, the puppies are starting to learn the scent and feel of their brothers and sisters. During this period, puppies learn to use their hearing to follow sounds and their vision to follow moving objects.

At this time, the puppies' mother begins the discipline process. Some people may try to stop the mother from correcting the puppies, but it is important not to interfere. The discipline doled out now will help each puppy accept training in the future. Through their mother, pups learn to accept a subordinate position in the pack. A mother's discipline at this stage of development also teaches the puppies to accept corrections, training, and affection.

Puppies should be socialized from an early age.

The breeder should be handling the puppies now to get them used to people. At this age, the puppies can learn the difference between their mother's touch and gentle human handling. A puppy who is denied the opportunity to interact with humans while young will have more trouble during the socialization process, which is discussed later in this chapter.

The Next Four Weeks

Puppies will develop significantly between five and seven weeks of age, learning to recognize the difference between dogs and people and starting to respond to individual voices. They are playing more with

Scary!

Sometime between 17 and 26 weeks, many puppies will go through another fear period and routine, everyday things may suddenly become frightening. Do not reinforce or encourage any of these fears by babying the youngster. Act exactly as you did when the dog was eight weeks old, and things will soon be back to normal.

Puppies should remain with the breeder until the fear period has passed.

littermates. Through this type of play, puppies are learning quite a bit about the world. They will learn how to play nicely with other dogs because they will surely be told by brothers, sisters, and mother when they are getting out of line. Although it may seem as if the puppies in a litter are fighting or playing too roughly, they are just trying to assert their personalities and discover how to be submissive and how to be dominant.

The eighth week is a frightening time for most puppies. This is the first of several periods of fear that they will go through during their early development. Puppies should not be taken from their mother between four and eight weeks of age. Those who go to new homes too early may have lasting behavior problems, such as difficulty dealing with other dogs, trouble accepting rules and discipline, and they may become

Puppies learn about the world through play.

excessively shy, aggressive, or fearful. For example, if puppies leave the breeder's home during this fear period and are taken to the veterinarian by the new owner, they may fear the vet for life. By leaving an eight-week-old puppy with the breeder, mom, and littermates for one or two more weeks, you can avoid any bad experiences that may form a lasting impression.

Leaving Home

The ninth and tenth weeks are the perfect time for puppies to go to their new homes. At this age, they are ready to form permanent relationships. Take advantage of this and spend time with your new puppy; play with the youngster and encourage him to explore his surroundings and to meet new people. During this time, you should begin socializing your pup, which is more than simply introducing him to other people, dogs, noises, and sounds. It is making sure that these things do not frighten your puppy as you introduce them. The period between the eighth and twelfth weeks is the most important for your puppy's socialization.

Dominance/Submission

It is important to establish dominance over your dog, especially during the difficult teen years. A human can express dominance or submission toward a dog in the following ways:

- ✓ Meet your dog's gaze; averting your gaze will signal submission.
- ✓ Stand above your dog; being at his level or lower would show submission.
- ✓ The owner should only pay attention when the dog obeys a command.
- ✗ Do not allow your dog to chase children or joggers.
- ✗ Do not allow your pup to jump on people or mount their legs. Even females may be inclined to mount, as it signals dominant behavior in a dog.
- ✗ Do not allow your dog to growl for any reason.
- ✗ Do not participate in wrestling or tug-of-war games.
- ✗ Do not physically punish your puppy for aggressive behavior. Prevent him from repeating the infraction and teach an alternate behavior.

Behave, or...

Behavior problems are the reason many pet owners remove dogs from their homes, as well as the main reason so many dogs end up in shelters or euthanized.

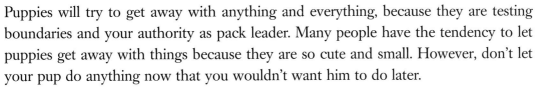

Don't let your dog engage in behaviors now that won't be acceptable later.

Discipline is also very important during this stage of development. Your puppy is trying to find a place in the family's pack order and needs to learn that there are specific rules that must be followed.

Puppies will try to get away with anything and everything, because they are testing boundaries and your authority as pack leader. Many people have the tendency to let puppies get away with things because they are so cute and small. However, don't let your pup do anything now that you wouldn't want him to do later.

Growing Up

From 13 through 16 weeks of age, your puppy will be trying to establish a position in your family pack. By now, your pup should have a good idea of what behaviors can and cannot be tolerated in his new home. Consistency is very important, and everyone in the family should enforce the household rules in the same way. Puppies are pretty intelligent and very aware of their surroundings and the dynamics that make up their family. If there is a weak link in the chain of command, your puppy will take advantage of it. As with children, a puppy will behave for Mom and not for Dad, or vice versa. Some puppies will treat children just like littermates and try to dominate them. Puppies with dominant personalities may start mounting behavior with small children in the family or may nip and wrestle with them. By this time, your puppy is well on the way

Discourage possessive behavior with a basic obedience command.

to establishing a spot in the social order. It is your job to make sure your pup knows that he comes after all the humans in the family.

Between four and six months of age, protective instincts will develop. If your pup begins to show protectiveness or aggression by growling, snarling, barking, or raising hackles, interrupt this behavior by distracting the dog and giving a basic obedience command that your pup knows well. If you encourage the behavior or correct it harshly, you will be placing too much emphasis on it. For some pups, any attention is good attention, even being scolded for misbehaving. Instead, remain calm and remind him that you are the leader of the pack.

The Terrible Teens

The teenage experience for a dog is very similar to that of a human adolescent's experience. A dog's teenage stage usually hits at about 12 months of age, although it's not unusual to see it develop a month or two earlier. You'll know when it happens. One day you will ask your previously well-trained, sweet little puppy to do something he knows very well, such as sit, and your dog will look at you as if he's never heard that word before.

Do you remember your own behavior during adolescence? Basically, it was impossible to believe that anyone could be more embarrassing than your parents. (It's amazing how smart they become once you are a little older!) It's this same attitude that affects teenage dogs. Teenagers (dogs and humans) are constantly striving to prove that they can take care of themselves. They want to be independent, yet they know that they still need the security of their parents' guidance. These conflicting needs seem to drive some teens (and their parents) crazy.

Similar to human teenagers, adolescent puppies push the boundaries of their rules and test their parents' limits. Many dogs at this age act as if they are entirely too cool to listen to you or to hang out with you. Another common teenage behavior includes a lack of manners. Your previously well-mannered puppy may not be able to talk back to you but may start barking at other dogs, jumping on people, or chasing cars.

During this stage of development, you will need to consistently enforce social and household rules. Hopefully, you and your dog will have already graduated from puppy kindergarten training, because that basic control will help. If you haven't started training by this point, now is the time to do so.

Make sure that your dog knows you are the leader. This is not the time to be best friends with your dog. If you become lax in your position as leader, any puppy with a dominant personality will regard you as a pushover and walk all over you. Instead, act like the leader you are. Don't allow any behaviors that you would normally not tolerate. Some owners see their dogs become dominant when they are allowed on the furniture or the bed, because the dog is then at the owner's level. If you reprimand your puppy for misbehavior, make sure that you are standing over him. An owner can gain dominance by ignoring all of the puppy's social initiatives. Dogs should earn everything they get from their owners. This would include sitting for petting or treats, sitting before going out the door, and sitting to receive a collar and leash. These exercises reinforce the owner's dominance. Most importantly, don't take it personally–this rebellion is not aimed at you. It is a very natural part of growing up, and it will pass in a

Attack Poodles?

One trainer told me about a problem she had with two Poodles, Sugar and Spice. They were as adorable and tiny as could be. Their owner figured that there wasn't any harm in letting them run everywhere and bark at everything. She even thought it was kind of cute when all five pounds of Sugar and Spice would protect the living room couch and maul whoever sat there—after all, what damage could they do? After six months of their constant barking and refusing to walk on a lead, the owner had two tiny, uncontrollable terrors and a living room she couldn't enter. She finally decided to seek professional help. The moral of the story is that no matter what their size, basic training is essential to help dogs develop into well-mannered adults who are pleasurable to live with.

Part 1

Different breeds display different behavioral characteristics.

Balloon-o-phobia

Socialization should include as many experiences as possible—even things that may seem perfectly harmless to you can frighten your puppy. My first dog, Sam, was deathly afraid of balloons and would bark, whine, and hide if one happened to float by anywhere in his territory. Apparently, a balloon had popped near him when he was a puppy and the fright left him with bad memories ever since. Needless to say, all birthday parties in my house were balloon-free!

few months, thankfully much quicker in dogs than in humans. Your puppy will eventually mature, and if you are consistent in training, the pup will turn back into that enjoyable friend you once had.

Canine Behavior

Canine behavior is both inherited and learned. Related breeds show tendencies toward certain behavioral characteristics. An experienced breeder should inform you of both the upside and the downside of the breed's personality. Unfortunately, some breeds are labeled with poor temperaments when actually only a small percentage of individuals in the breed have a problem. If there are good temperaments in the background of the pup you have chosen, there is an excellent chance that he will have a good temperament as well. Many temperament or behavior problems are simply due to lack of training or socialization.

Many of us do not realize that our dogs make amazing sacrifices to fit in with human society. In many cases, we tend to forget that dogs are just that–dogs, not human beings. The more you learn about canine behavior, the better you can understand the motivation behind some of your puppy's actions. Once you understand the motivation, it will be easier to correct unwanted behavior and mold your pup into an asset to your family and society in general.

Understanding the Dog's Language

Dogs cannot talk–and most dog owners often wonder what they might say if they could. Unfortunately, this obstacle can sometimes make it difficult for both parties to get their points across. It's hard for the puppy to understand what the owner wants, and it's hard for the owner to know what the puppy can understand.

Dogs communicate through body language, not only within the pack but with outsiders as well. They also put in a lot of effort to try to understand the things we teach them. The least you can do is try to understand what your pup is telling you. If you can read your puppy's body language, it will be easier for you to communicate with him.

Classifications of Canine Posture
(Tuskegee University, 1993)

Attentive: Ears up; eyes moving; lips relaxed; head up; hair down; weight equally distributed; tail stiff, horizontal, and moving slowly; no verbal communication

Playful: Ears up; eyes moving; lips relaxed; hair down; leaning back, weight shifted to rear; front foot may wave at target; tail wagging high, broad, and fast; animated, exaggerated, bouncing movements; may bark, pant, or whine

Aggressive: Ears forward at first, out and down as he escalates, back when attacking; eyes fixed, staring at target; lips raised, mouth slightly open; nose wrinkled; head high; hair raised over rump and back of neck; leaning forward, weight shifted to front; body stiff and tense; front leg may point at target; tail stiff and high over back; lip may quiver; may growl, snarl, and bark

Submissive: Ears down; eyes down; lips down, retracted horizontally; head down; hair down; leaning back, weight shifted to rear; tail may wag horizontally, hang down, or be tucked close to body; may whine

Passively Submissive: Ears down; eyes down; lips down; hair down; head down; lying on side or back; tail tucked close to body; may urinate

Fearful: Ears back and down; eyes wide opened and fixed; mouth open slightly; head down; hair raised over neck; leaning back, weight shifted to rear; tail tucked tight under abdomen; may tremble and defecate; makes fast moves if threatened; looks for an escape route; whines

Eye contact is one way the alpha wolf keeps order within the pack. You are the alpha, so the first step is to establish eye contact with your puppy. Practice maintaining eye contact, even if you need to hold your dog's head for five to ten seconds at a time. Never look away first, and always reward with a treat and praise when the pup submits to you. Make sure your eye contact is gentle and not threatening. Later, if your dog has been naughty, it is permissible to give a long, penetrating look. This is usually much more effective when disciplining your dog than any physical punishment could ever be.

Your puppy will also display different postures that have very specific meanings in the canine world. If you are aware of these postures, you can tell exactly how your dog is feeling.

Puppy Socialization

What Is Socialization?

Throughout this chapter and others, the importance of socializing your puppy is discussed. It figures into every aspect of your puppy's care and training. What exactly is socialization? In terms of puppy raising, socialization refers to the process of introducing your pet to the surrounding environment and life among people. A puppy cannot recognize or feel comfortable around unfamiliar people or situations. A puppy who has the opportunity to meet all kinds of people–people of different ages, sizes, shapes, and races–will be less likely to be afraid or aggressive toward them. For example, a puppy who has never met an elderly person might shy away from one later in life. Dogs should also meet as many different types of animals as possible. If your puppy learns to tolerate the neighborhood cat without too much fuss, he will be less likely to chase it.

Socialization should include an introduction to everything that is part of your world–water, trees, plants, loud noises, vacuum cleaners, stairs, toys–everything! The more things your pup experiences pleasantly, the less he will be afraid of later.

The Importance of Socialization

Socialization will give your puppy the skills to cope with the world. When dogs are isolated from people at an early age, especially during the all-important first 8 to 12 weeks of life, they will never be able to form a strong attachment to people. Instead of feeling like part of the human pack, they will feel threatened and aggressive toward anyone who approaches.

A puppy can inherit a bad temperament from one or both parents and will consequently not make a good pet or working dog. However, bad temperament can also be caused by a lack of socialization or mistreatment. A bad-tempered dog will never become an asset to society, but in fact is a liability and will often have to be euthanized.

How to Socialize Your Dog

The first step in getting a stable, well-adjusted companion is obtaining a happy puppy from a breeder who is determined to produce dogs with good temperaments. Such a person has taken all the necessary steps to provide early socialization. The puppies should be kept in an environment where they are able to see and be around people, and they should be handled

Socialization is an integral part of raising a puppy.

Solitary Confinement

The worst thing that you could do is purposely not socialize a dog in order to create a better watchdog. A properly socialized dog will instinctively know the difference between an accepted person and an intruder. Ignoring the socialization process will only increase the chances of your puppy becoming too aggressive or unstable, perhaps resulting in euthanasia. Even working guard dogs eventually go off duty and need to know how to behave with the friendly people around them.

regularly. If your breeder has children, even better–this gives the puppies a chance to meet gentle children in the first weeks of life. Socializing with humans is critical up through 12 weeks of age. If puppies are not socialized with people by then, they will

Socialization with humans is critical through 12 weeks of age.

Socialization Don'ts

✗ Don't overwhelm your puppy with lots of new things at once. Socialization should take place gradually.

✗ Don't force your puppy to approach things that he is afraid of, as it will only make the situation worse.

✗ If he is frightened of something, don't reinforce fears by coddling or encouraging him to be frightened in any way.

✗ Don't let people overstimulate the puppy. (Children are especially guilty of this.) Make sure you supervise the pup around new people and give plenty of "down" time for puppy relaxation.

✗ Don't let people surprise your puppy or handle him too often. A pup should explore the environment at his own pace.

✗ Don't socialize your puppy without vaccinations.

be timid in later life. A puppy should stay with his dam and littermates until at least seven or eight weeks of age, because the interaction with siblings will help when meeting other dogs.

Once you bring your puppy home, continue the socialization started by the breeder. You should introduce your puppy to everyone you can. If you have young ones in your family, teach them to treat the puppy with respect. If you do not, find some *gentle* children to play with your puppy. Energetic kids make wonderful playmates for the energetic puppy, and vice versa. Introduce the pup to everyone in the neighborhood–the mail carrier, the police officer, the gas station attendant, an elderly neighbor, and anyone else who may come knocking on your door. Practice teaching your puppy good manners while you make introductions. Now is a good time for him to practice sitting for attention and for you to control barking or aggression. Reinforce your alpha role. Your puppy has no choice but to accept these strangers because you say so. Let each person give a treat (that you provide) when the dog behaves. After a while, your pup will be thrilled to meet anyone you care to introduce. The best way to socialize a dog is to visit as many different places as you can, like the beach, the park, and the store.

Expose your pup to different noises and situations, such as busy streets or crowded pet stores—always *on lead*, of course. Introduce him to other well-socialized dogs; puppies must learn to get along with other dogs as well as with humans. Find a puppy kindergarten class in your area and attend regularly. Not only is it a great place to socialize your dog, it is also the first step in training the new addition to your family.

Teach your dog good manners when making introductions.

Starting Over

Perhaps you have taken home an older puppy or adult dog from a shelter, and you do not have firsthand knowledge of previous socialization. Perhaps you already know that the dog has been mistreated or neglected when very young. All is not lost; there are plenty of things that you can do to get your puppy on the right track.

First, you need to inquire about the puppy's social experience and find out as much as you can about his early weeks of life. Kennel dogs may have a difficult time adjusting to people and environmental stimuli. Some puppies have been mistreated, and this fear or resentment will linger. For example, if your puppy was mistreated by a woman, he may prefer men. Some dogs may hold a grudge against everyone in uniform. Perhaps

Part 1

Your puppy should interact with other well-socialized dogs.

Training reinforces your position as pack leader.

your puppy is afraid of water, the car, or loud sirens. These fears can probably all be traced back to a traumatic experience in the formative weeks of life.

You need to approach these problems very gradually and carefully, especially if your dog is aggressive toward people. Do not throw your puppy at the very thing that is frightening; that will only make the situation worse. Introduce kind, gentle people to your puppy slowly and in small increments. For example, if your puppy is afraid of the mail carrier, take him out on lead when the mail is delivered. With the mail carrier's permission, of course, be reassuring and have your pup sit when the carrier approaches. Act perfectly normal toward the person, carry on a brief conversation, and then have the mail carrier give your puppy a treat. Do this over a period of weeks. By now, your pup should at least be able to control these fears and not act shyly or aggressively. Do the same for any frightening situation.

Basic training is also very helpful. Performing commands gives your puppy something to concentrate on and reinforces your position as the leader of the pack. This should be reassuring and make your dog feel more comfortable in any situation.

Your puppy may never get over some fears entirely, but with careful conditioning and training, he should be able to cope with daily activities without problems. If your puppy is not responding and is still acting aggressively, you may need to consult an experienced trainer for professional advice.

Forming a Bond

Dogs are extremely sociable by nature. Because of their pack mentality, they like to be surrounded by the people who are most important to them and are unhappy if they are left out. While caring for and playing with your pup, you are forming a deep and long-lasting emotional bond with another living creature, which is beneficial on numerous levels.

Owning a dog helps improve the quality of our lives. Seeing to a dog's daily care encourages an owner to think of things that otherwise may

Playing with your dog will strengthen the bond between the two of you.

MY 4-Legged Child?

Studies on the human/animal bond illustrate the importance of the unique relationships between people and their pets. Those of us who share our lives with pets understand the special part they play through their companionship, service, and protection. For many, the pet/owner bond goes beyond simple companionship; pets are considered members of the family. A leading pet food manufacturer recently conducted a nationwide survey of pet owners to gauge just how important pets were in their lives. Here's what they found:

76% allow their pets to sleep on their beds

78% think of their pets as their children

84% display photos of their pets, mostly in their homes

84% think that their pets react to their own emotions

100% talk to their pets

97% think that their pets understand what they're saying

seem unimportant. For example, senior citizens show more concern for their own eating habits when they have the responsibility of feeding a dog. The older owner may not be getting enough exercise or outside time, but when responsible for a dog, that formerly sedentary person has a reason to get up and get moving.

Over the last few decades, it has been shown that pets relieve stress. Owning a pet has been known to lessen the occurrence of heart attack and stroke. Also, many single people thrive on the companionship of a dog. Pets can provide people with a sense of purpose and make them feel needed.

The majority of our dogs live in family environments. The companionship they provide is well worth the effort involved. Children benefit from the opportunity to have a family dog. Dogs teach children to take responsibility for living things and help them to have empathy and respect for animals. Children and dogs sometimes seem as if they were made for each other, and the special friendship that develops between them is an experience that should not be overlooked.

Owning a pet has been shown to relieve stress.

The potential of the bond between humans and animals is still being explored, and new discoveries are made every day. Today, more dogs are helping thousands of people as service dogs. Also, dogs are able to perform many different tasks for their owners. Search and rescue dogs, with their handlers, are sent throughout the world to assist in the recovery of disaster victims. Therapy dogs are very popular with nursing homes, and many hospitals allow dogs to visit their patients. People truly look forward to their visits and feel better physically with a dog in their beds to hold and love.

You have made the decision to bring a puppy into your home–don't miss out on the best part of dog ownership. The love and affection that you give to your dog will be returned to you a million times over.

Today, therapy dogs are very popular in nursing homes and hospitals.

Part Two
Your Healthy Puppy

"You're going to be OK, Mr. Sparky. Just take two bones and call me in the morning."

Health Care

There are few things sadder than a sick puppy. Luckily, you can ensure your puppy's good health by being a responsible owner and providing everything needed to maintain his well-being. Your puppy cannot take himself to the veterinarian, set up an inoculation schedule, check for parasites, or handle an emergency. This is all up to you. The better care you take of your puppy now, the longer you'll have a wonderful companion. Remember, a healthy puppy is a happy puppy!

How to Recognize a Healthy Puppy

Your puppy should be the picture of good

The better care you give your puppy now, the healthier he'll be as an adult.

Choosing a vet takes time and research.

health and appear vibrant, alert, and interested in the world. Check your pup's body on a regular basis. If you know how things look when they are normal, it will be easier for you to detect any abnormalities that might occur.

Veterinary Care

Choosing your pup's "personal physician" takes time and research. The vet will be one of the most important people in your puppy's life, so choose carefully. In this section, we will discuss your pup's basic veterinary requirements in more detail. Statistics show that two out of three pets will experience major medical problems in the course of their lifetime. The high cost of some veterinary procedures, which can run into thousands of dollars, has forced owners who may not have the money into making tough choices, watching their pets suffer, or euthanizing them. To help defray expenses,

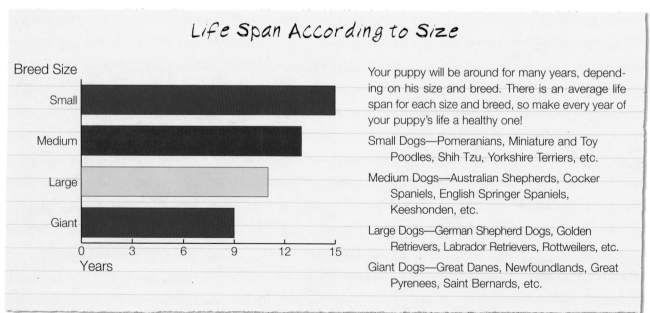

Life Span According to Size

Your puppy will be around for many years, depending on his size and breed. There is an average life span for each size and breed, so make every year of your puppy's life a healthy one!

Small Dogs—Pomeranians, Miniature and Toy Poodles, Shih Tzu, Yorkshire Terriers, etc.

Medium Dogs—Australian Shepherds, Cocker Spaniels, English Springer Spaniels, Keeshonden, etc.

Large Dogs—German Shepherd Dogs, Golden Retrievers, Labrador Retrievers, Rottweilers, etc.

Giant Dogs—Great Danes, Newfoundlands, Great Pyrenees, Saint Bernards, etc.

more and more owners are turning to pet insurance. There are several companies that offer this type of insurance.

The First Checkup

You will want to take your new puppy for a first checkup within 48 to 72 hours after bringing him home. A puppy can appear healthy at first but may have a serious problem that is not immediately apparent. Many pets have some minor condition that may never become a real problem. Unfortunately, if the dog does have a serious problem, you may want to consider returning the pet, especially if you have children, because attachments will be formed that may have to be broken prematurely.

At the first visit, the veterinarian will check your pet's overall health, which includes listening to the heart; checking the respiration; feeling the abdomen, muscles, and joints; checking the mouth, including the gum color and signs of gum disease, as well as plaque buildup; checking the ears for signs of an infection or ear mites; examining the eyes; and last but not least, checking the condition of the skin and coat.

Health Check

A healthy dog should display these characteristics:

- ✓ Eyes—Bright, clear, and free of redness, discharge, or inflammation
- ✓ Nose—Moist, not dry or cracked, and free of discharge
- ✓ Ears—Should look clean and smell pleasant with no soreness or redness
- ✓ Mouth—Fresh breath and firm, pink gums with no redness or bleeding; no broken or missing teeth
- ✓ Body—No indication of pain or tenderness; no lumps, bumps, or red spots
- ✓ Anal area—Clean and free of any debris; anal sacs on either side of the anus should not be swollen
- ✓ Coat—Free from mats and any other debris, like flea dirt (little black specs); skin should not appear dry or flaky
- ✓ Legs—No pain or stiffness
- ✓ Feet—No lumps, sores, burrs, or any other foreign objects; pads should be examined for cuts and nails checked for length

If you perform an all-over exam on a daily basis, it will be easy to spot any problems before they become serious.

Next, your vet will discuss the proper diet and the quantity of food to give your puppy. If this is different from your breeder's recommendation, then you should discuss those

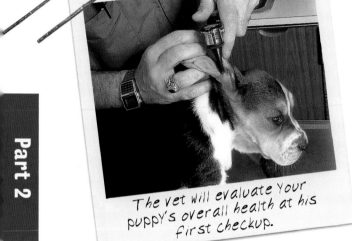

The vet will evaluate your puppy's overall health at his first checkup.

Vaccination Motivation

Although there are potential problems with some vaccines, vaccinations have saved countless dogs from deadly diseases that would have caused death in the past. If you are concerned about certain vaccinations or schedules, discuss them with your veterinarian and come to a solution that will safeguard your puppy's health.

suggestions with your vet as well. If you decide to change the diet, it should be done over a prolonged period of time so as not to cause gastrointestinal upset.

It is also customary to take a small stool sample to test for intestinal parasites. It must be fresh, preferably within the last 12 hours, because the eggs hatch quickly and may not be observed under the microscope. If your pet won't oblige, the technician can usually take one in the clinic.

Immunizations

It is important to take your puppy's vaccination record with you on your first visit. Presumably, the breeder has started the puppy on a vaccination schedule that is current to the time you acquired the dog. Your puppy has probably received vaccinations for distemper, hepatitis, leptospirosis, parvovirus, and parainfluenza every two or three weeks from the age of five or six weeks. This is usually a combined injection, typically called the DHLPP. Why are so many immunizations necessary? No one knows for sure when the puppy's maternal antibodies are gone, although it is generally accepted that distemper antibodies are gone by 12 weeks. Parvovirus antibodies are usually gone by 16 to 18 weeks of age. However, it is possible for the maternal antibodies to be eliminated earlier or later. Therefore, immunizations are started at an early age. Vaccines will not provide immunity while maternal antibodies still exist.

Canine Diseases

Distemper

Distemper is often a fatal disease. If a puppy does recover, he is subject to severe nervous disorders. The virus attacks the entire body and resembles a bad cold with a fever. It can cause runny nose and eyes and gastrointestinal disorders, including a poor appetite, vomiting, and diarrhea. The virus is

Choose your puppy's veterinarian carefully.

Part 2

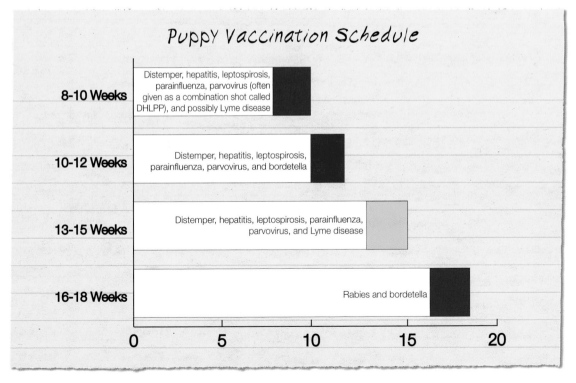

Puppy Vaccination Schedule

Age	Vaccinations
8-10 Weeks	Distemper, hepatitis, leptospirosis, parainfluenza, parvovirus (often given as a combination shot called DHLPP), and possibly Lyme disease
10-12 Weeks	Distemper, hepatitis, leptospirosis, parainfluenza, parvovirus, and bordetella
13-15 Weeks	Distemper, hepatitis, leptospirosis, parainfluenza, parvovirus, and Lyme disease
16-18 Weeks	Rabies and bordetella

0   5   10   15   20

An annual physical is good preventive medicine.

carried by raccoons, foxes, wolves, mink, and other dogs. Unvaccinated puppies are very susceptible.

Hepatitis

The hepatitis virus is most serious in very young dogs. It is spread by contact with an infected animal through feces or urine. The virus affects the liver and kidneys and is characterized by high fever, depression, and lack of appetite. Recovered animals may be afflicted with chronic illness.

Leptospirosis

Leptospirosis is a bacterial disease transmitted by contact with the urine of an infected dog, rat, or any other wildlife. It produces severe fever, depression, jaundice, and internal bleeding and was fatal before the vaccine was developed. Recovered dogs can be carriers, and the disease can be transmitted from dogs to humans. Unfortunately, there are several strains of leptospirosis, and vaccinations usually protect against only two.

Check This

Health care does not end with vaccinations. It is very important to take your dog to the vet for an annual checkup, which includes booster vaccinations, a check for intestinal parasites, and a blood test for heartworm. The annual physical is good preventive medicine. Through early diagnosis and subsequent treatment of potential problems, your dog can maintain a longer and better life.

Parvovirus

Parvovirus was first noted in the late 1970s and can still be a fatal disease. However, with proper vaccinations, early diagnosis, and prompt treatment, it is manageable. It attacks the bone marrow and intestinal tract. The symptoms include depression, loss of appetite, vomiting, diarrhea, and collapse. Immediate medical attention is essential.

Rabies

Rabies is shed in an animal's saliva and is carried by raccoons, skunks, foxes, other dogs, and cats. It attacks the nervous system, resulting in paralysis and death. Rabies can be transmitted to people and is virtually always fatal. The only true test for rabies involves euthanizing the animal.

Bordetella (Kennel Cough)

The symptoms of bordetella are coughing, sneezing, hacking, and retching accompanied by nasal discharge usually lasting from a few days to several weeks. There are several disease-producing organisms responsible for this illness. The present vaccines are helpful but do not protect against all strains. It usually is not life threatening, but in some instances, can progress to bronchopneumonia. The disease is highly contagious, and the vaccination should be given routinely to dogs that come into contact with other dogs through boarding kennels, training classes, or visits to the groomer.

Coronavirus

Coronavirus is usually self-limiting and not life threatening. It was first noted in the late 1970s, about a year before parvovirus. The virus produces a yellow/brown stool and may be accompanied by depression, vomiting, and diarrhea.

Lyme Disease

Lyme disease was first diagnosed in the US in 1976 in Lyme, CT, in people who lived near areas that had deer ticks. Symptoms may include acute lameness, fever, swelling of joints, and loss of appetite. Your veterinarian can tell you if you live in a high-risk area.

Pet Insurance

Veterinary Pet Insurance (VPI) is the largest, with more than 850,000 clients. It operates just like a human health care insurance plan. Owners can go to any licensed veterinarian, veterinary specialist, or animal hospital in the world. To find out more about pet insurance, ask your veterinarian, call VPI at 800-872-7387, or visit the Web site at www.veterinarypetinsurance.com.

Part 2

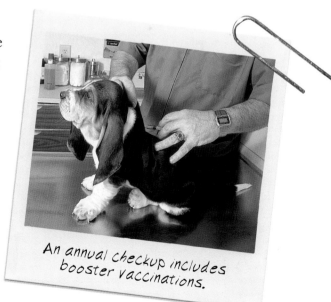

An annual checkup includes booster vaccinations.

How to Get Rid of Fleas

✓ Vacuum rugs and furniture to get rid of flea eggs. Change the vacuum bag often so fleas are not deposited back into the area later.

✓ Treat the area with flea killer.

✓ Wash the dog's bedding and blankets in hot soapy water and wash out all crates, doghouses, toys, etc. with disinfectant.

✓ Sweep all uncarpeted areas, including porches, sidewalks, and patios.

✓ Treat your yard with flea killer.

✓ Give your puppy a bath and apply topical flea preventative.

✓ Remember to reapply flea preventative to your dog as recommended.

Boosters

After your puppy has completed the basic series of vaccinations, you should continue with a DHLPP booster once a year. Some veterinarians recommend a rabies booster one year after the first inoculation and then every year or every three years, depending on your local laws. The Lyme disease and coronavirus vaccines are given annually, and it may be recommended that bordetella prevention be given every six to eight months.

External Parasites

There are many types of external parasites, and your puppy is susceptible, especially if he spends a lot of time outdoors or around other pets. The best way to deal with these buggy creatures is to keep one step ahead of them at all times. Be vigilant about checking your pup's coat, especially after he's been playing outside. There are also products on the market available through your veterinarian that will keep the creepy crawlers away. An ounce of prevention is worth a pound of cure–this is especially true when it comes to keeping your pup bug-free.

Fleas

These pests are not only a dog's worst enemy but also an enemy to you, your house, your yard, and your pocketbook. Once fleas infiltrate the area, they can be very difficult to get rid of. Many dogs are allergic to a fleabite, and in some cases, it only takes one fleabite to start an allergic reaction. This can result in open sores or fleabite dermatitis. A heavy infestation of these pests can cause blood loss and then anemia, which can be fatal to tiny pups. Preventing flea infestation is the key.

If there is a flea infestation, no one product is going to correct the problem. Not only

Part 2

MY Dog Has Fleas?

If you aren't sure if your dog has fleas, place the pup on a solid, light-colored sheet or blanket. Comb the dog's coat thoroughly, especially around the stomach, the armpits, and around the tail. (These out-of-the-way places are where fleas like to hide.) Then let him up. If there is any residue on the sheet, the brush, or the comb that looks like salt (which are flea eggs) and pepper (which are flea dirt or fecal matter), your dog has fleas.

Treat fleas under your veterinarian's guidance.

will the dog require treatment, but so will the environment. However, some products are not usable on young puppies, and treating fleas should be done under your veterinarian's guidance. Treat all pets in your household at the same time, because fleas are easily passed from one to the other.

Adult fleas live on the dog, but their eggs drop off of the dog into the environment. There they go through four larval stages before reaching adulthood, when they are then able to jump back on your unsuspecting puppy. The cycle resumes and takes between 21 to 28 days under ideal conditions. Several environmental products are available that will kill both the adult fleas and the larvae. Use a spray designed for outside use in the yard and a spray designated for inside use in your home. Carefully follow the directions on any product that you use.

Ticks

Ticks are known carriers of disease for both animals and humans. They carry Rocky Mountain Spotted Fever and Lyme disease and can cause tick paralysis. These eight-legged oval insects will bury their heads in your puppy's skin and live off his blood. You

Taking Your Puppy's Temperature

The normal canine temperature is 99.5 to 102.5°F. Taking your dog's temperature is a good way to detect illness. To take your puppy's temperature accurately, use a rectal thermometer. Obviously, it is best to buy one for canine use only. Lubricate the tip of the thermometer using petroleum jelly. Kneel alongside your puppy or place him on your lap. Lift the tail gently and rotate the thermometer gently into the rectum, only going in about an inch or two. It will take two minutes to get an accurate reading on a regular thermometer (less time with a digital), so praise and distract your puppy until time is up. If the temperature is too high or low, call your veterinarian and report your readings, along with any other symptoms.

can remove them with tweezers, using a slow, twisting motion, and pulling out the head. Although using a flea-preventative can help repel some ticks, it is not totally effective. Dogs should be checked for ticks regularly, especially if they have been in wooded areas or tall brush.

Sarcoptic Mange

The mite characterized by sarcoptic mange is difficult to find on skin scrapings. The female mite burrows under the skin and lays her eggs, which hatch within a few days. Sarcoptic mange causes intense itching in dogs and may even be characterized by hair loss in its early stages. Sarcoptes are highly contagious to other dogs and to humans, although they do not live long on humans.

Demodectic Mange

This mite is passed from the dam to her puppies. It often affects youngsters from three to ten months of age. Diagnosis is confirmed by skin scraping. Small areas of hair loss around the eyes, lips, and/or forelegs become visible. There is little itching unless there is a secondary bacterial infection.

Cheyletiella

This causes intense itching and is diagnosed by skin scraping. It lives in the outer layers of the skin in dogs, cats, rabbits, and humans. Yellow-gray scales may be found on the back and the rump, top of the head, and the nose of dogs who are suffering from this particular type of mange.

Ringworm

Ringworm isn't really a worm but rather several different kinds of fungi that can affect dogs and humans. These very contagious fungi infest the skin and cause round, scaly, "ring-like" areas that are very itchy. Because this is so contagious, immediately take your puppy to the vet for treatment and follow directions exactly to prevent the fungus from spreading.

Intestinal Parasites

Worms–yuck! Yes, internal parasites are disgusting and can also be extremely dangerous for your puppy. They can be found in very young puppies, because many are passed from mother to offspring, either in the womb or through nursing. They are also dangerous because you can't actually see all of them, and many times pups will not show any obvious symptoms until very ill.

Intestinal parasites are more prevalent in some areas than others. Climate, soil, and contamination are big factors that contribute to the incidence of intestinal parasites. How does your puppy get these things? A dog with worms may defecate in the local park. Eggs are passed in the stool. Dogs sniff or walk through the feces and may get some on their coat or feet and lick it off. The best chance of your puppy remaining worm-free is to regularly pooper-scooper your yard and watch out for

> ### Heartworm
>
> Incidents of heartworm have been found in all 50 states. According to the American Heartworm Society, the highest infection rate in dogs occurs within 150 miles of the Atlantic and Gulf coasts and along the Mississippi River.

Intestinal parasites are more prevalent in some areas than others.

etc.) for their breed. Reputable breeders do not want the dogs they produce to be bred indiscriminately–an important concept. More and more effort is being made to breed healthier, better dogs.

Shelters and humane societies require that you spay or neuter your puppy because they see firsthand how vast the problem of pet overpopulation is and wish to spare any resulting puppy of such litters the pain of being placed in a shelter.

When to Spay/Neuter

You should spay your female pup at around six months of age. There are numerous benefits to this. Unspayed females are subject to mammary and ovarian cancer. In order to prevent mammary cancer, a female should be spayed prior to her first heat cycle. Later in life, an unspayed female may develop a pyometra, a uterine infection, which is a life-threatening problem. Spaying is performed under a general anesthetic and is easy on the young dog. As you might expect, it is a little harder on an older dog, but that is no reason to deny your older girl future good health. The surgery removes the ovaries and uterus. It is important to remove all the ovarian tissue. If some is left, your dog could remain attractive to males.

Neutering the male at a young age will inhibit some characteristic male behavior that owners frown upon. Some boys may not lift their legs and mark territory if they are neutered at six months of age. Also, neutering at a young age has other benefits, such as lessening the chance of hormonal aggressiveness. Surgery involves removing the testicles from the scrotum. If your male has a retained testicle either in the abdomen or inguinal canal, he needs to be neutered before the age of two or three years. Unneutered males are at risk for testicular cancer, perineal fistulas, perianal tumors, and prostatic disease.

Intact males and females are prone to housetraining accidents as well. Females urinate more frequently before, during, and after heat cycles, and males tend to mark territory if there is a female in heat. Males may show the same behavior to a visiting dog or guests. Spaying or neutering curbs these behaviors and promotes good health.

Recognizing Trouble

Most puppy owners are lucky; their pups live healthy lives and never require more than an annual trip to the veterinarian for booster shots. But dogs, like all other animals, may contract problems and diseases that need professional treatment. It is a very bad idea to attempt to diagnose a problem without the advice of a veterinarian. A relatively common problem, such as diarrhea, might be caused by nothing more than a puppy pigging out on leftovers or eating something unusual. Conversely, it could be the first indication of a potentially fatal disease. Your veterinarian is the only one qualified to make the correct diagnosis. Taking your puppy to the veterinarian is the most responsible and humane thing you can do for your dog. He will thank you for it.

Your vet is the only one qualified to make the correct diagnosis.

The following symptoms, especially if they accompany each other or progressively add to earlier symptoms, indicate that you should visit the veterinarian right away:

Vomiting

All puppies vomit from time to time, and it is not necessarily a sign of illness. However, continued vomiting is a clear sign of a problem. It may be a blockage in the pup's intestinal tract, it may be induced by worms, or it could indicate any number of diseases.

Your pet will benefit from quality health care.

If your pup displays signs of illness, take him to the vet.

Diarrhea

Many factors, including change of environment, change of diet, or stress, can cause diarrhea. If it lasts more than 48 hours or if blood is seen in the feces, something is wrong and your puppy should be taken to the vet immediately.

Running Eyes and/or Nose

If your pup's eyes and nose are weepy, they should quickly clear up if the puppy is placed in a warm environment and away from any drafts. If they do not, and especially if a mucous discharge is seen, these symptoms must be diagnosed by your veterinarian.

Respiratory Problems

Prolonged coughing, wheezing, or any other indication that your puppy is having trouble breathing is a sign of a problem. Check for a blockage, then immediately call your veterinarian.

Crying When Eliminating

This might be a minor problem caused by constipation, but it could be more serious and indicative of an internal infection or blockage, especially if the pup cries when urinating as well.

Crying When Touched

Obviously, a puppy might yelp if you do not handle him with care. However, if your dog cries even when lifted gently, there may be an internal problem that becomes apparent when pressure is applied to a given area of the body. If there is also an extended abdomen, pain, or lameness in any of the joints, take your pet to the vet.

Refusing Food

Generally, puppies are greedy creatures and will eat almost anything you offer. Some may be fussier than others, but no puppy will usually refuse more than one meal. If your pup goes for a number of hours without showing any interest in food, then something is decidedly behind this behavior and the dog should be taken for an examination.

Fainting or Seizures

Seizing or fainting can indicate a number of disorders, some very serious. If your puppy has a seizure or suddenly collapses, first prevent the pup from being injured as best you can; then contact your vet immediately.

Eye Injuries

If your puppy suffers from any sort of eye injury, your veterinarian should be contacted immediately.

Take your dog to the vet if he displays unusual behavior.

Cuts or Wounds

Most cuts or scrapes can be easily treated by washing the affected area and applying an antibiotic ointment. However, if your puppy has suffered a wound that will not stop bleeding with direct pressure, you need to go to the veterinarian for further treatment.

Allergic Reactions

If your puppy swells up (especially in the face) or becomes ill after eating something or receiving a bite or sting from another animal or insect, you are probably seeing an allergic reaction. Seek treatment as soon as possible.

Good health care will ensure a happier, healthier puppy.

General Listlessness

All puppies have days when they do not seem their usual energetic, mischievous selves. However, if your puppy seems overly tired, restless, or aggressive, or is displaying unusual behavior, like hiding from you, then there is a problem. This general malaise or change in personality may or may not accompany other symptoms. There are many diseases that can develop internally without displaying obvious clinical signs. Blood, fecal, and other tests are needed in order to identify the disorder before it reaches an advanced state.

Giving Medication

It can be very frustrating to try to get your squirmy little pup to swallow a pill, but it is not impossible. Following are a few tips that can help make it easier for everyone.

When giving a pill, never underestimate the power of treats. Many dogs love cheese, so wrap the pill in cheese and your dog will probably wolf it down. If cheese isn't your dog's weakness, almost anything else will work. Peanut butter, bread, a bit of hot dog, or a soft dog biscuit are good hiding places for pills.

Liquid medicine can be a little harder. It is easiest to use a syringe into which the medication can be measured. Place the tip into the side of your puppy's mouth by the back teeth. Squirt the medication in, and then hold your puppy's muzzle shut so that he cannot spit it out; stroke your dog's throat so that he will swallow.

Eye medication should be given as quickly as possible. Give the puppy something to occupy him, hold his head, spread the eyelids, and apply the medication.

Dental Care

Your new puppy comes with a brand new set of puppy teeth. Anyone who has ever raised a puppy is abundantly aware of these teeth—he will chew anything, chase your shoelaces, and play with every piece of clothing.

Newborn puppies have no teeth. At about four weeks, puppies begin to get their deciduous or baby teeth. They begin eating semi-solid food, play-fighting with their littermates, and learning discipline from their mother. As their new teeth come in, their mother's feeding sessions become less frequent and shorter. When pups are six to eight weeks of age, the mother will start growling to warn them when they are fighting too roughly or nursing too hard, causing her pain with their new teeth.

At about four months of age, most puppies begin shedding their baby teeth. Often these teeth need some help coming out to make way for the permanent teeth. The incisors (front teeth) will be replaced first, then the adult canine or "fang" teeth. When a baby tooth is not shed and a permanent tooth comes in, veterinarians call it a retained deciduous tooth. This can cause gum infections by trapping hair and debris between the permanent tooth and the retained baby tooth.

Puppies need to chew, as it is a necessary part of their physical and mental development. They develop muscles and life skills as they drag objects around and fight over possessions. Puppies chew on things to explore their world and use taste to

> ## CRT
>
> It is important to know how gums look when your dog is healthy so you can recognize potential problems. There are one or two breeds, like Chow Chows, that have black gums and a black tongue, which is normal for them. Generally, however, a healthy dog will have bright pink gums. Pale gums are an indication of shock or anemia and should be considered an emergency. Likewise, any yellowish tint is an indication of a sick dog. To check a dog's capillary refill time (CRT), press your thumb against the gums. The gum will turn white but should refill and turn to normal color within one or two seconds. Your pup's CRT is very important—if the refill time is slow and the dog is feeling poorly, you should call the veterinarian immediately.

Part 2

Yearly veterinary dental exams are essential.

Regular brushing promotes healthy teeth.

determine what is food and what is not. Good chew toys can help clean puppy teeth while alleviating the need to chew. Puppies who have adequate chew toys will have less destructive behavior, have better physical development, and have less chance of retaining deciduous teeth.

During the puppy's first year, your veterinarian should inspect your dog's lips, teeth, and mouth as part of a regular physical examination. As mentioned in the grooming section of this book, you should help maintain your dog's oral health. Examine your puppy's mouth at least weekly throughout the first year to make sure there are no sores, foreign objects, tooth problems, etc. Excessive drooling, head shaking, or bad breath are trouble signs, so consult your veterinarian. By six months of age, all of his permanent teeth are in, and plaque can start to accumulate on the tooth surfaces. This is when your dog needs good dental care to prevent calculus buildup. Regular brushing, along with safe chew toys, are the best ways to take care of your puppy's teeth.

By the time dogs reach four years of age, 75 percent have periodontal disease. It is the most common infection in dogs. Yearly examinations by your veterinarian are essential to maintaining healthy teeth. If periodontal disease is detected, your veterinarian may recommend a prophylactic cleaning. To do a thorough cleaning, it will be necessary to put your dog under anesthesia. Your veterinarian will scale the teeth with an

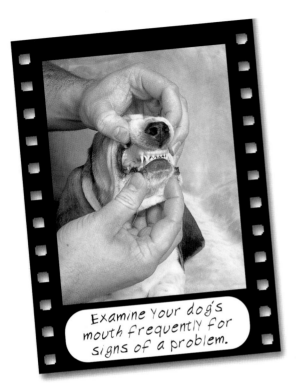

Examine your dog's mouth frequently for signs of a problem.

Chew toys can help clean your dog's teeth.

ultrasound scaler or hand instrument, removing the calculus. If the periodontal disease is advanced, the veterinarian may prescribe a medicated mouth rinse or antibiotics for use at home.

As your dog ages, professional oral examinations and cleanings should become more frequent. Your senior dog's mouth should be inspected at least once a year, and eventually your vet may recommend visits every six months. Dogs with good chewing habits as puppies will have healthier teeth throughout their lives.

Puppy First Aid

It is a good idea to always be prepared for an emergency. As you may well know, puppies are ingenious at getting into any and all sorts of trouble. Even if you have puppy-proofed your house as recommended, there is always the possibility that something may happen. Always keep a first-aid kit nearby, and have the numbers of your veterinarian, emergency clinic, and poison control center near the telephone.

There are things that you can do to help your dog if he ever suffers from any of the following problems.

Puppies are ingenious at finding trouble.

Cardiac Arrest

If you realize that your dog is not breathing, you should have someone call the veterinarian and plan for transportation to an emergency facility immediately. If your dog does not have a heartbeat or spontaneous respiration, you can perform CPR.

CPR may help save your puppy's life. This will require two people—one person to breathe for the dog and the other to try to establish a heart rhythm. Mouth-to-mouth resuscitation requires two initial breaths, one to one-and-a-half seconds in duration. After the initial breaths, breathe for the dog once after every five chest compressions. To do this, inhale, cover the dog's nose with your mouth, and exhale gently into the dog's mouth. You should see the dog's chest expand. Sometimes, pulling the puppy's tongue forward stimulates respiration. You should ventilate the dog 12 to 20 times per minute.

The person who is managing the chest compressions should make sure that the dog is lying on his right side and should place one hand on either side of the dog's chest directly over the heart (between the fourth and fifth ribs, usually at the point of the flexed elbow). The number of chest compressions administered depends on the size of the patient—about 80 compressions per minute for a puppy. Check for spontaneous heartbeat and/or respiration while you are performing CPR, and if they are present, discontinue resuscitation and monitor the patient.

Bleeding

Bleeding can result from any accident, such as a ripped dewclaw, a toenail cut too short, a puncture wound, or

Puppy First-Aid Kit

Before you bring your puppy home, you should put together a first-aid kit, which should include:

- ✓ Vital information card: phone numbers for vet, clinic, etc.
- ✓ A muzzle—pantyhose or stretchable gauze could make a muzzle
- ✓ Scissors
- ✓ Tweezers
- ✓ Eyewash
- ✓ Antibiotic ointment or powder
- ✓ Hydrogen peroxide
- ✓ Milk of magnesia
- ✓ Thermometer
- ✓ Petroleum jelly
- ✓ Gauze rolls
- ✓ Adhesive bandaging tape
- ✓ Cotton balls
- ✓ Antibacterial soap
- ✓ A blanket or towels
- ✓ Rubbing alcohol

a laceration. If your puppy is bleeding, apply a clean pressure bandage and check every 15 to 20 minutes to ensure that it is not too tight. Styptic powder can stop the flow of blood from a small cut on the dewclaw or toenail. Clean the wound with antiseptic. If the wound is deep or does not stop bleeding, take your pup to the veterinarian immediately.

Shock

Shock is a life-threatening condition that requires immediate veterinary care. It can occur after an injury or a severe scare. Other causes of shock are hemorrhage, fluid loss, infection, poison, adrenal insufficiency, cardiac failure, and anaphylaxis. The symptoms are a weak, rapid pulse, shallow breathing, dilated pupils, low temperature, and muscle weakness. The puppy's capillary refill time (CRT) will also be slow. Keep the dog warm and go to the veterinary clinic immediately. Timing is critical to survival.

Choking

If your dog is choking, see if any foreign object is visible. If so, remove it. If no object is visible, you can perform the Heimlich maneuver on your dog. Wrap your arms tightly around your dog's belly just under the rib cage. Give one quick forceful squeeze, and the object causing the obstruction should be expelled.

Heart Rate, Pulse, and Respiration

You can take your dog's heart rate by pressing your fingertips on his chest. Count for ten seconds and then multiply by six to obtain the rate per minute. Normal heart rates range from about 50 beats per minute in the larger breeds to 130 beats per minute in the smaller ones. A normal pulse rate is the same as a heart rate and is taken at the femoral artery, which is located on the insides of both rear legs. Respiration should be observed, and depending on the size of the dog, should be about 10 to 30 breaths per minute.

Most accidents require immediate veterinary care.

Part 2

Supervise your dog when he is around water.

Car Problems

Although it's been said many times before, many people don't realize how quickly a car can overheat, even with the windows cracked open. Never leave a dog unattended in a car. Also, short-nosed breeds, like Bulldogs and Pugs, and obese or infirm dogs should not be left outside for long periods in hot weather and should only exercise in the early morning or evening when the temperature is cooler.

You can also try holding the puppy upside down to see if the object will become dislodged. Meanwhile, have someone call the veterinarian.

Drowning

Remove any debris from the puppy's mouth and swing the dog, holding him upside down. Try to stimulate respiration by pulling the tongue forward. Administer CPR if necessary and call your veterinarian. Do not give up working on your dog, and go to the vet as soon as possible. Be sure to wrap the dog in blankets or towels to prevent shock.

Heatstroke

Heatstroke is a serious emergency–and can usually be prevented. Dogs are not able to cool off by sweating as humans can. Their only way to cool off is by panting and radiation of heat from the skin's surface. When exposed to high temperatures, high humidity, or poor ventilation, dogs can suffer from heatstroke very quickly, especially brachycephalic (short-nosed) breeds, like Bulldogs or Pugs.

The signs of heatstroke are rapid, shallow breathing, rapid heartbeat, a temperature above 104°F, and collapse. The dog needs to be cooled down as quickly as possible and treated by a veterinarian. If possible, spray your pup with cool water or cover him with cool, wet towels. Pack ice around the head, neck, and groin, and let the dog slowly drink cool, not cold, water. Monitor his temperature and stop the aforementioned procedure as soon as the temperature reaches 103°F. However, continue monitoring, because you do not want it to elevate again or drop below 100°F. The best thing to do for your puppy is to get professional help as soon as possible.

Poisoning

Hopefully, you have followed this book's advice and have sufficiently puppy-proofed your home. However, puppies do have a way of getting into things that they shouldn't.

If your puppy eats or drinks something poisonous, call your vet immediately. Be prepared to give the weight and age of your puppy and the quantity of toxin consumed, and have the bottle handy to read off the ingredients. If you can't reach the vet, you can call the National Animal Poison Control Center.

Symptoms of poisoning include muscle trembling and weakness, increased salivation, vomiting, and loss of bowel control. There are numerous household toxins, plants, and pesticides that can be harmful to your puppy, so be sure to keep a careful eye and act immediately if you suspect he has eaten something poisonous.

Seizure

Some dogs are prone to seizures, which may also be a secondary symptom of an underlying medical condition. Make sure the dog is in a safe place and cannot hurt himself. Do not try to handle the dog's mouth or you may get bitten. Notify your veterinarian if your puppy has a seizure, fit, or convulsion of any kind so he can be checked for further problems.

Toads

Toads are poisonous if ingested and quite deadly to dogs. You should find out if these critters live in your area and what they look like.

Foreign Objects

There is one thing that puppy owners will learn very quickly—it doesn't have to be food for your puppy to swallow it. Dogs have been known to swallow anything, including socks, clothing, pantyhose, toys, and plastic. Sometimes these items may pass through the puppy's body without incident, but other times he may not be so lucky. The object may get stuck in the intestinal tract or stomach and sometimes needs to be removed surgically. If you suspect that your puppy has swallowed a foreign object, contact your veterinarian. Depending on what it is, the vet may either tell you to induce vomiting or to come to the clinic for further treatment. Don't induce vomiting until you talk to your vet—some objects may do more damage coming back up.

Part 2

Bites

If your dog gets bitten, try to stop any bleeding, wash the area, and determine the severity of the situation. Some bites may be superficial and easily treated, while others may need immediate attention. However, most should be seen by a veterinarian, and some may require antibiotics or stitches.

Accidents

Many traffic accidents can be easily prevented by making sure that your puppy is always in a fenced area or on leash. If an accident does occur, remember not to panic. First, get your dog to a safe area. He may be in pain or in shock, so make an emergency muzzle so you don't get bitten while you are trying to help. Is the dog conscious or unconscious? Are there any obvious injuries, like bleeding or broken limbs? Even if there are no obvious injuries, your dog may still be injured internally.

Try to get another person to help you lift the dog onto a blanket, but with no more movement than absolutely necessary. Use the blanket as a stretcher, and carry the dog to your car for immediate transport to your veterinarian or emergency clinic. Even without external injuries, the dog should still be x-rayed for broken bones or internal damage.

How to Make an Emergency Muzzle

An injured dog may be frightened or in pain and may not even recognize his owner. Use an emergency muzzle to protect yourself from being bitten when you try to help.

- ✓ Use a strip of cloth, bandage, nylon stocking, or leash to make a muzzle quickly.
- ✓ Make a large loop by tying a loose knot in the middle of the strip of cloth.
- ✓ Hold the ends up, one in each hand.
- ✓ Slip the loop over the dog's muzzle and lower jaw, just behind the nose.
- ✓ Quickly tighten the loop so that the dog's mouth cannot open.
- ✓ Tie the ends under the lower jaw.
- ✓ Make a knot and pull the ends back on each side of the face and under the ears to the back of the head.

Try practicing this when your dog is calm and not injured so that you are ready for any emergency.

Electrocution

Unfortunately, puppies have been known to chew on electrical wires and get a shock. If this happens, turn off the current before touching the dog. Check for a normal heart rate and that the dog is breathing. Administer mouth-to-mouth resuscitation or CPR if necessary. Go to the veterinarian as soon as possible, because electrocution can cause internal damage that will need medical treatment.

Walks on the Wild Side

Every now and then, your puppy could have a run-in with another animal–and the outcome may not be pleasant. The following information will help if your puppy has a problem with a member of another species:

Protect your pet from outdoor dangers.

Bee Stings

Bees and wasps will leave an embedded stinger in your puppy's skin. Remove the stinger with tweezers and apply ice if the area swells. Some people swear that a paste of baking soda and water will help to ease discomfort; others use milk of magnesia or ammonia to soothe the area. Some dogs will have an allergic reaction to bee stings and will experience severe swelling in the face or throat. If this happens, urgent medical care is necessary.

Snake Bites

It is good to know if any poisonous snakes are in your area so that you can be extra careful when walking with your dog. If your puppy is bitten and exhibits any swelling, trembling, drooling, vomiting, excitability, dilated pupils, or collapses, apply

Dog Bites

If your puppy gets bitten by another dog, it is very important to find out if the other dog has had rabies vaccinations. If the offender is a stray, try your best to confine the dog for observation. All dog bites should be reported to the local Board of Health.

Prickly Situation

When removing porcupine quills, make sure that you get all of them out–some quills may be small and get lost under your pet's coat. Feel your dog's muzzle carefully for any that may be hiding under the skin. If you can't remove all of the quills, take your puppy to the vet right away.

an ice pack to the wound and do your best to stem the flow of blood if there is any. If the bite is on the leg, apply ice and wrap a bandage tightly around the wound. Contact your veterinarian at once.

Skunks

Most puppies will investigate anything. Your puppy's curiosity will be peaked by that black-and-white animal over there, and next thing you know–skunked! First, don't let your dog inside the house–that smell can be almost impossible to get rid of. Check the pup's eyes for any redness or irritation, and if there is any, wash the eyes with cool water. Then it's bath time, preferably outside under the garden hose. Shampoo and rinse him thoroughly. Unfortunately, this is sometimes just not enough to get rid of the odor. Pet owners recommend rinsing your dog with tomato juice; medicated douches (2 ounces mixed with 1 gallon of water); or a solution of 1/4 cup of baking soda, 1 teaspoon of liquid soap, and 1 quart of hydrogen peroxide.

Porcupine Quills

Having a run-in with a porcupine can be one of the biggest mistakes your puppy may make. Porcupine quills have backward pointing scale-like hooks that hold them firmly in the flesh, making them painful and difficult to remove. If your puppy has been really pricked, it is best to go to the vet to get them removed. A vet may administer anesthetic so the dog may escape some of the pain. You can try to get the quills out yourself if there are only a few. Wear rubber gloves to protect your hands and try to soothe your puppy–these things really hurt! With a pair of needle-nose or blunt-nose pliers, grab a quill as close to the dog's coat as possible. Pull steadily until it comes out. Once you get the quills out, apply a topical antiseptic to prevent infection.

Feeding and Nutrition

As a puppy owner, you'll discover that the one thing your puppy loves the most (besides you, of course) is food. Good nutrition is a necessary requirement in a puppy's life. Providing your puppy with the proper diet is one of the most important aspects of dog care. By carefully researching which diet is best for your puppy, you can ensure your dog's good health.

A Puppy's Nutritional Needs

Puppies may have individual nutritional needs depending on the breed group to which they belong. Each breed has different activity levels,

Good nutrition is crucial to a puppy's development.

Due to their high energy demands, the Sporting Group needs extra calories.

hereditary conditions, genetic makeups, and original function, so each will require a specialized diet to fit these needs.

The Sporting Group

As a whole, this group needs extra calories for energy and performance. You should look for a dog food with higher amounts of vitamin and mineral fortification, as well as choline to help process nutrients into energy. Some Irish Setters are gluten intolerant, which can cause weight loss and diarrhea. Grains containing gluten—like wheat, barley, and oats—should be eliminated, and rice should be used as a substitute.

Also, Cocker Spaniels and some Golden Retrievers suffer from a low taurine level that can be responsive to supplementation. Several sporting breeds suffer from hip dysplasia. Slowing down the dog's growth rate as a puppy has a positive impact in reducing this hereditary disease.

Bloat

Bloat (gastric dilatation-volvulus) is a life-threatening veterinary emergency that usually occurs when a dog swallows a large amount of air while eating or exercising. It causes the stomach to twist, trapping fluids and gas within it. Deep-chested breeds and large- or giant-sized dogs are most susceptible, such as the Great Dane, German Shepherd Dog, and Saint Bernard. Signs that your dog may be bloated include retching without vomiting, excessive salivation, weakness, swelling of the abdomen, abnormal rapid breathing, and increased heart rate. Because death can occur within hours, rush your puppy to the vet immediately if you see these symptoms.

The exact cause of bloat is not known, but controlling your dog's food intake can help. Feed several small meals throughout the day instead of one large meal, and don't let your dog exercise one hour before or after eating.

They're Sweet Enough!

It may seem harmless to feed your puppy sweets, but chocolate can cause your dog to become seriously ill or even die. The two chemicals in chocolate, caffeine and theobromine, overstimulate the puppy's nervous system, especially in small dogs—10 ounces of chocolate can kill a 12-pound dog! Symptoms of chocolate poisoning include restlessness, vomiting, increased heart rate, seizure, and coma. If your dog has ingested chocolate, you can give syrup of ipecac at 1/8 of a teaspoon per pound to induce vomiting, and get your puppy to the veterinarian immediately.

Will Work for Food

For puppies, food can be an important and effective training tool. A treat can be just the right motivation to encourage your pup to sit, come to you, follow you on leash—almost any behavior is more fun with a treat for a reward. Food also establishes your dominant position over the puppy. If you remember to make your puppy sit or wait before diving into the food bowl, you will be recognized as pack leader.

The Hound Group

This group is prone to intestinal problems and requires a highly digestible diet. A diet high in ground rice, oats, and barley can help provide a balance of fiber and carbohydrates to improve gastrointestinal health. Also, small hounds, like Beagles and Dachshunds, can suffer from bone and joint problems as well as obesity.

When you purchase your puppy, make sure the breeder discusses all the health problems that exist in the breed along with what you can do to nutritionally manage potential health problems.

The Working Group

This group commonly encounters heart and gastrointestinal problems, as well as bone and joint difficulties. Choose a dog food that is restricted in salt for heart health and that is high in

The Working Group needs a dog food that is high in fiber.

Dalmatian puppies need a low-purine diet.

Herding dogs require an abundance of protein.

fiber for digestibility. These breeds can also suffer from hereditary bone diseases like hip dysplasia. Again, slowing down the dog's growth as a puppy can help reduce the symptoms of these conditions.

The Terrier Group

Terriers are basically healthy dogs, but they require a lot of protein if they live a high-performance lifestyle. In this group, 75 percent of all Bedlington Terriers suffer from copper toxicosis or are genetic carriers of it. If your Bedlington puppy carries this disease, you must discuss with your breeder or veterinarian the best way to manage the copper levels in his diet.

The Toy Group

Due to their small size, the breeds in the Toy Group have their own set of problems that can be managed nutritionally. In general, small dogs put out more body heat per unit of body weight than larger breeds. By managing the levels of protein, you can make the most of your toy dog's food intake for energy. Toy dogs, especially Yorkshire Terriers, often suffer from hypoglycemia, or low blood sugar. Maintaining blood sugar levels can reduce the incidence of this problem.

The Non-Sporting Group

A generous supply of vitamins A and B and minerals such as copper and zinc can help this group of dogs that often suffers from skin and hair coat conditions. Dalmatians tend to have uric acid calculi problems, so puppies should be given a low-purine diet.

(Purines are a type of protein known to promote urinary stones in Dalmatians.) Breeds like Poodles and Bichon Frises tend to have problems with periodontal disease, so special care should be taken to feed them kibble to help reduce tartar buildup.

The Herding Group

This group needs an abundance of protein because it uses up a lot of energy in its everyday work. Hip dysplasia is prevalent in several breeds, such as the Collie and the Shetland Sheepdog, and slowing down the puppy's growth rate can help reduce the symptoms. Also, German Shepherd Dogs tend to suffer from chronic intermittent diarrhea resulting from an intestinal immune deficiency, so fat calories should be monitored carefully.

Dog Foods

If you take a trip to your local pet emporium or supermarket, you cannot help but notice that there is an overwhelming selection of dog foods available. It can be confusing, to say the least, and makes it hard to choose which brand is best for your puppy. There are certain things you should know about commercial dog foods that will help you make the right decision. The more you educate yourself about what your puppy's nutritional needs are and how dog food is manufactured, the easier the decision will be.

Good Food for Good Health

In order to stay healthy, there are six essential nutrients that all dogs in every stage of life need in varied

Got Beef?

Unlike cats, dogs are not true carnivores and can exist on a vegetarian diet. They can convert vegetable fat and protein into the ingredients that they need to perform bodily functions. However, you should consult a veterinarian before switching your dog to a vegetarian diet, because it is a lot of work to maintain balanced nutrition.

Part 2

Dogs should eat food that will ensure proper nutrition.

What Is in This Stuff?

Element	Function	Source	Diet Deficiency Indications
Protein	Proteins can be burned as calories and stored as fat. They help with muscle growth, tissue repair, blood clotting, and the immune system.	Meat, fish, poultry, milk, cheese, yogurt, fishmeal, and eggs.	Weight loss, dull coat, a depressed immune system, and poor growth result if the diet is lacking in protein.
Fat	Fat supplies energy needed for the absorption of certain vitamins, provides insulation from the cold, and makes food tastier.	Meat, meat by-products, and vegetable oils such as safflower, olive, corn, or soybean.	Dull coat and delayed healing of wounds result if the diet is lacking in fat.
Carbohydrates	Carbohydrates provide energy and keep intestines functioning smoothly. Complex carbohydrates are fiber and sugar.	Corn, oats, wheat, rice, and barley.	Possible fertility and whelping problems may result if the diet is lacking in carbohydrates.
Vitamins	Vitamins are divided into two groups: water soluble and fat soluble. Water-soluble vitamins pass through the body in urine. Fat-soluble vitamins are stored in body tissue and can become toxic in excessive amounts. Vitamin A protects skin and promotes bone growth; vitamin B aids in metabolism, vitamin D aids in bone growth and increases calcium absorption; vitamin K helps with blood clotting.	Fruits, vegetables, cereals, and the liver of most animals.	Skin thickening, nerve decay, heart failure, weight loss, anorexia, anemia, scaly skin, fatty liver, rickets, muscle weakness, infertility, or hemorrhage may result if the diet is lacking in vitamins.
Minerals	Minerals provide strength to bone, ensure proper bone formation, maintain fluid balance as well as normal muscle and nerve function, transport oxygen in the blood, and produce hormones.	Calcium, phosphorus, copper, iron, magnesium, selenium, potassium, zinc, and sodium are essential minerals.	Poor growth, rickets, convulsions, anemia, hair loss, lethargy, kidney problems, or muscle weakness result from mineral deficiency.
Water	Water is the most important nutrient and makes up over 60 percent of a puppy.	Water intake can come directly through drinking or can be released in the body when food is oxidized.	Dehydration, which can lead to serious deterioration of organs and even death, results from insufficient amounts of water.

amounts: protein, fat, carbohydrates, vitamins, minerals, and water.

Types of Dog Food

Pick a dog food specially formulated for puppies that will ensure the proper nutrition for the pup's developing organ systems. There are three types of dog food available–dry, canned, and semi-moist–and all of them have good and bad points. You must choose the type that best fits your puppy's needs.

Reading Labels

There are two agencies that work together in regulating pet food labels. The first agency, the Association of American Feed Control Officials (AAFCO), is a non-governmental agency made up of state and federal officials from all over the United States. It establishes pet food regulations that cover areas like guaranteed analysis, nutritional adequacy statements, and feeding directions. Each state decides whether or not to enforce AAFCO's regulations. Most do; however, some do not.

Of Chicken Lips & Pig's Wings

What exactly are meat by-products and meal? Actual meat is considered to be the clean flesh of a slaughtered mammal and is limited to the part of the striated muscle that is skeletal or found in the tongue, diaphragm, heart, or esophagus. Meat by-products are the non-rendered lean parts other than the meat, which include but are not limited to the lungs, spleen, kidney, bone, blood, stomach, intestines, necks, feet, and undeveloped eggs. Meat and bone meal are the rendered product or mammal tissue, which include bone, hair hood, horn, hide trimming, manure, and stomach. The ingredients in dog food can vary widely, so be informed about what your puppy is actually eating.

Part 2

The second agency, the Food and Drug Administration Center for Veterinary Medicine, establishes and enforces standards for all animal feed. This federal agency oversees aspects of labeling that cover proper identification of product, net quantity statements, and the list of ingredients.

Learn how to read dog food labels. Slight changes in wording can make the difference between a quality dog food and one that may not be what it seems.

Product Name

Specific words used in the name can indicate what is in the food and what is

Food Facts

Type	Upside	Downside
Dry Food	Least expensive, can be left in bowl for longer periods of time, and helps control tartar.	Least appealing to dogs.
Canned Food	Most appealing to dogs.	Spoils quickly, expensive, and requires more to be fed because energy content is relatively low, especially for large breeds.
Semi-Moist Food	Will not spoil at room temperature and comes in prepackaged servings.	Contains large amounts of sugar and preservatives in order to maintain freshness without refrigeration.

not. For example, a name like "Beef Dog Food" must contain at least 95-percent beef, but if it is called "Beef *Formula* for Dogs," it is required to contain a minimum of only 25-percent beef. Other words like dinner, platter, nuggets, or entrée fall under this 25 percent minimum requirement.

Another word to watch for is "with." A dog food called "Dog Food With Beef" must contain only a minimum of 3-percent beef. The word "with" was originally supposed to highlight extra ingredients, but recent amendments to AAFCO regulations now allow the word to be used in the product name. The word "flavored" can be deceiving, because it means that only a sufficient amount of flavoring needs to be added for it to be detectable. "Beef-Flavored Dog Food" may not include any beef at all and may only be flavored with very small amounts of beef by-products.

Ingredient List
Each ingredient contained in the food will be listed in descending order according to weight, but the quality of the ingredient is not required to be listed. For the best results, look for animal-based proteins to be high on the list, such as beef, beef by-products,

chicken, chicken by-products, lamb, lamb meal, fish meal, and egg. However, read carefully, because some manufacturers will manipulate the weight of products in order to place them higher or lower on the list. For example, they may divide the grains into different categories, like wheat flour and whole ground wheat, in order to lower the weight and make it seem less prominent on the ingredient list.

Guaranteed Analysis

The guaranteed analysis states the minimum amount of crude protein and crude fat, as well as the maximum amount percentage of moisture (water) and crude fiber. The word "crude" refers to the method of testing the product, not the quality of the nutrient. Sometimes,

Feeding nutritious foods will result in a healthier dog.

Part 2

Feeding Do's and Don'ts

✓   Do provide puppy food made from a reputable manufacturer.

✓   Do have fresh water available for your puppy at all times.

✓   Do serve your puppy's food at room temperature.

✓   Do watch your puppy's weight.

✓   Do call your veterinarian if your puppy refuses to eat in a 24-hour period.

✓   Do feed your puppy nutritious snacks.

✗   Don't allow children to interfere while the puppy is eating.

✗   Don't offer spoiled or stale food to your puppy.

✗   Don't change your puppy's diet suddenly.

✗   Don't leave any uneaten canned or moist food out after your puppy is finished eating. Discard dry food at the end of each day.

✗   Don't allow your puppy to have brittle bones or unhealthy snacks.

✗   Don't feed your puppy first. Eating after you will help to establish your dominant role.

Truth in Advertising

Although dog food labels tell you a lot about a product, there is a lot they don't tell you. For example, some wording used on labels can be misleading. Foods that use the words "gourmet" or "premium" are not required to contain any higher quality ingredients than any other product. Products that claim to be "all-natural" are not required to be. Some might think that this means the food is minimally processed or contains no artificial ingredients, but this is not necessarily true. In fact, all dog foods must contain some chemically synthesized ingredients in order to be deemed complete and balanced.

manufacturers will list other nutrients like ash or calcium, although they are not required to do so.

Nutritional Adequacy Statement

This statement is important because it states what life stage the product is formulated for, such as growth, reproduction, maintenance, senior, or all life stages. For developing puppies, look for the product that is especially formulated for growth. It should also tell you whether the product is "complete and balanced" or "complementary." Complete and balanced means that it contains all the ingredients that your dog will need on a daily basis and it can be a meal by itself. Complementary means that it is not intended to be used alone and must be added to another product to create a complete meal.

Net Quantity Statement

The net quantity statement shows the weight of the food in the bag or can in pounds and ounces as well as metric weight. Be careful, because some companies use 30-pound bags and then only put 25 pounds of food inside.

Feeding Instructions

The feeding instructions on the dog food label are only suggestions; some dogs will eat more, some will eat less. Also, they are the amounts needed for the entire day, so you can divide it up the best way for your puppy. If you are not sure how much to feed, start off with the suggested amount and increase or decrease as necessary.

Homemade Diets

There seems to be a debate about whether a homemade diet is better for your dog than manufactured dog food. The downside to a homemade diet is that you need to

Supplements

Healthy puppies who are fed a balanced diet will not need supplements. In fact, some veterinarians believe that supplementing your puppy's diet with extra vitamins and minerals can aggravate conditions like hip dysplasia and hereditary skin problems. The only time you should give your puppy any kind of supplements is under the direction of your veterinarian, and even then you should never exceed the prescribed amount.

Make sure you are providing your dog with all the required nutrients.

Part 2

be very careful to ensure that you are providing your puppy with all the required nutrients. It also takes a lot of time, effort, and energy to cook a proper diet for your dog on a daily basis.

Those who are in favor of a homemade diet believe that commercial dog foods contain contaminated and unhealthy ingredients and feel that it is worth the effort to give their puppy a home-cooked meal. If you have the time and the money and believe that it is important to feed your dog a homemade diet, consult your veterinarian, who can give you a reputable and nutritionally balanced recipe. Although millions of dogs exist and stay healthy on commercially prepared dog food, the ultimate decision is yours.

Now that you have learned all you can about dog food and feeding options, you can make an informed choice about what to buy for your puppy.

Feeding Your Puppy
First Meals

If you are lucky, the breeder from whom you obtained your puppy will have given you a diet sheet, which will help you immensely with your feeding chores. A diet sheet will

Follow the directions on the dog food label for feeding amounts.

quickly to the schedule, and you'll have more control over the amount consumed.

How Much to Feed

If you don't know the puppy's prior feeding schedule, you will have to figure out how much to feed him. Start by following the directions on the dog food label and increasing or decreasing the amount as needed. Put down the recommended amount for your puppy's age and take it away after a period of time. If your puppy eats the food quickly and leaves nothing, you need to increase the amount. If there is leftover food, you may have to decrease the amount or feed smaller meals more frequently.

Giving your puppy the proper amount of food is very important, especially for large- or giant-breed puppies. These dogs, who are usually over 65 pounds when mature, can suffer from skeletal abnormalities, such as hip dysplasia, hypertropic osteodystrophy, and osteochondritis dessecans if they grow too fast. These problems are characterized by improper development of joints or bones and can cause lameness. Some researchers also say that too much calcium in a puppy's diet can interfere with normal bone and cartilage development.

Large-breed puppies need to receive the proper amount of food.

Although these problems have a lot to do with heredity, they can be nutritionally managed. Be sure to talk with your breeder and your veterinarian about how to handle these problems if you have any questions.

Although they are not as susceptible to orthopedic problems, medium-sized to small-sized breeds also need to have their weight monitored. All puppies can get obese if they eat too much, which can lead to health problems. Small breeds can also suffer from low blood sugar levels. All dogs need to have a nutritionally balanced diet in order to stay their healthiest.

Treats and Bones

Treats are a great way to encourage and reward your puppy for doing something well. There are plenty of treats available today that are not only tasty but also nutritious. Hard biscuits can help keep puppy teeth clean. Remember to consider treats as part of the dog's total food intake. Limit the amount of treats and be sure to feed only healthy snacks. Avoid giving table scraps, because they usually just add to caloric intake. Obesity is a very serious health problem in dogs, so be sure to start your puppy off eating right.

Bones can help your puppy with the overwhelming need to chew. They will also keep his teeth clean and prevent him from becoming bored. Make sure you give your dog safe bones and toys that are made specially for dogs and that will not splinter or break into tiny pieces, which can be swallowed and become stuck in the intestinal tract or choke the pup. There are plenty of manufacturers that make safe, chewable, edible dog bones, so give your puppy something fun and safe as a special treat.

Monitor the weight of your small- or medium-sized puppy.

Treats are a great way to reward your dog.

Part 2

Grooming Your Puppy

Puppies rely on their owners to keep them clean and brushed, which can be done easily with regular grooming. Grooming is also important because it gives you a chance to inspect your dog and catch any skin or health problems before they start. Every dog, no matter what breed, will require grooming, and some breeds require more attention than others. Hopefully, you have put some thought into the amount of time that you want to spend grooming your dog before you chose him and have taken home a breed that has the best coat type for you.

Every breed of dog will require grooming.

Each breed has a different coat type that makes it unique.

Wire Stripping

Wiry coats, like those of terriers, must be hand stripped every three to four months, which means pulling out the dead hair. It can be pulled out with your thumb and finger in the direction of growth, or you can use a stripping knife. If done correctly, it should not hurt the dog at all. It does take practice, however, so it may be wise to have a professional groomer who has worked on wiry coats show you how it's done or have the groomer do it for you. However, if you do not plan to show your wiry-haired dog, he can be groomed with a clipper.

Each breed has a different coat that gives it a certain "look" and sets it apart. There are lots of different looks from which to choose.

Coat Types

Short, Smooth Coat–Doberman Pinschers, Pugs, and Basenjis have this coat type, which lies close to the body.

Short, Wiry Coat–Wirehaired Dachshunds, all three Schnauzers, and most terriers have this type of coat, which is thick, hard, and bristly.

Short, Double Coat–The dog with this type of flat coat has straight, coarse hair on the outside and a soft, thin undercoat beneath it. Labrador Retrievers, smooth Chow Chows, and Rottweilers have this type of coat.

Long, Double Coat–The dog with this type of coat has a long, straight, coarse outercoat and a very thick undercoat. Samoyeds, Chow Chows, and Collies have long, double coats.

Long, Coarse Coat–Shih Tzu, Lhasa Apsos, and Tibetan Terriers have this type of coat, which has a softer undercoat mixed into the long, coarse coat.

Curly Coat–Bichon Frises and Poodles have this type of coat, which has thick, dense curls.

Long, Silky Coat–This type of coat is very fine and has little or no undercoat. Yorkshire Terriers, Maltese, and Silky Terriers have this coat type.

Hairless Coat–Some dogs, including the Chinese Crested and Xoloitzcuintli, are hairless. Despite the lack of coat, they have very sensitive skin and need special attention.

Grooming Tools Every Owner Should Have:

Pin Brush

This has long, straight metal pins attached to a rubber backing and is used mostly on longer-haired breeds.

Slicker Brush

The wire bristles grasp and remove a dog's undercoat, helping to reduce shedding; it keeps the coat from becoming matted.

Flea Comb

This is helpful in getting hard-to-reach spots and removing fleas or flea dirt.

Grooming Glove

This is great for dogs with short coats to loosen any dead hair and get rid of surface dirt.

Nail Clippers

Your dog has nails. You need these.

Doggy Toothbrush and Toothpaste

Be sure to use toothpaste and toothbrushes that are made specifically for dogs.

Shampoo

If you are unsure about what brand to buy, ask your breeder or veterinarian for a recommendation.

Conditioner

As with shampoos, your breeder or vet can recommend a brand that is right for your dog.

Electric Clippers

Some breeds, like Poodles, have coats that need to be clipped every six to eight weeks.

Scissors

Blunt-nosed scissors are handy for trimming excess hair on feet, legs, tail, or anal region, as well as for trimming his whiskers.

Part 2

Of course, different coat types require different levels of care. The short coats will require little more than a daily brushing and an occasional bath; the longer coats or wiry coats may require special grooming procedures. Each dog needs a different amount of time and energy spent on grooming. But remember, everything sheds to some degree.

To keep your dog looking good, you need the right tools. There is a large selection of grooming equipment available for every coat type, but there are some universal tools that every owner should have for general grooming.

Dry Ideas

If your dog has a long or clipped coat, you may want to use a hair dryer. Remember to always use a hair dryer on a warm or cool setting—never hot. Your pup's skin can easily burn from the high temperature. While drying, brush the hair straight away from the body.

Begin grooming
your dog during
puppyhood.

The Road to Beauty

Puppyhood is the best time to start grooming procedures, because your dog will become used to the grooming routine and soon come to expect it as part of everyday life. This is especially true if you have a dog who requires extensive grooming or if you plan to show him. It is best to start out slowly so that the dog doesn't become overwhelmed or frightened, and then build on grooming time until you have the whole routine down pat.

If your puppy requires lots of grooming time, it is best to invest in a good grooming table. Your dog's leash can be attached to the grooming arm on the table, which will help keep him secure. Most tables also have non-skid pads on the surface to keep the dog from sliding around. A grooming table will save your back as well, because it can be adjusted to your height and prevent you from having to bend over or kneel down.

Introduce the grooming table slowly. Place the pup on the table a few times without doing any grooming, but do offer a treat. After you do this a few times, your puppy should eagerly get up on the table. Then you can start lightly brushing him and running any appliances like hair dryers or clippers before actually doing any major grooming. When the dog seems totally comfortable, you can start grooming on a regular basis. This gradual introduction will ensure that your puppy grows to enjoy grooming time with you.

Brushing

Brushing your puppy on a daily basis will maintain his good appearance, reduce shedding, keep mats to a minimum, and allow you to inspect the coat for any foreign debris or skin problems. It also stimulates your dog's skin and spreads the coat's natural oils, which help keep a coat shiny and the skin healthy. Puppies who are brushed on a routine basis will need to be bathed less often, because most of the dirt and debris in the coat will be removed regularly.

Each coat type will require a different amount of brushing. Dogs with short or smooth coats, such as hounds, can be gone over with a grooming glove a few times a week; however, a dog with a long coat will need daily brushing to keep mats away.

Most dogs will thoroughly enjoy the time spent being pampered by you every day. What puppy can resist lounging on his owner's lap while being brushed–it's a canine paradise!

Bath Time

The trick is to make it as fun and rewarding as possible for your puppy. One owner always leaves treats on the sides of the tub and lets his dog eat them while being bathed. Now all he has to say is "Bath time," and the dog jumps right in.

Part 2

How to Bathe Your Puppy

Step 1: Brush out your puppy's coat and remove all mats.

Step 2: Plug your puppy's ears with cotton balls.

Step 3: Place a non-slip rubber mat on the floor of the tub, sink, or plastic bathtub.

Step 4: Soak the coat thoroughly with warm water.

Step 5: Using canine shampoo, and avoiding the head, work up a good lather against the natural direction of the coat.

Step 6: Carefully wash your dog's face with a washcloth, making sure not to get soap in his eyes.

Step 7: Rinse the coat thoroughly until all the soap is out.

Step 8: If you use a canine conditioner, massage and rinse the coat as you did using the shampoo.

Step 9: Squeeze the excess water from the coat and towel dry the dog. Let the dog shake the excess water out of his coat. Remove the cotton balls.

A Word of Warning: Just-bathed puppies will find the dirtiest spot in which to roll around, so it may be wise to keep them inside until totally dry.

Most puppies need to be bathed only occasionally.

Nail trimming is essential for your dog's safety and comfort.

Bathing

Most puppies will require a bath only occasionally. Healthy dogs are pretty good at keeping themselves clean, and regular brushing should keep your puppy's coat in good shape. Some dogs, like the Chesapeake Bay Retriever and the Great Pyrenees, have waterproof coats, and it is best not to bathe them too often because it can strip the natural oils and reduce the coat's ability to repel water. In fact, overbathing your dog can cause dry skin and irritation, which in turn causes excess scratching or infections. But every puppy, at some time or another, will roll in something particularly smelly or dirty and require a bath.

Toenail and Foot Care

Your puppy's feet really take a beating. They endure the pounding of all that puppy energy and traverse the terrain of every place he explores—over rocks, cement, wood, snow, or grass, your pup's feet get there first and suffer the hardest.

Always examine your puppy's feet as part of his daily grooming routine. Inspect your dog's feet after each outing and check that there are no sharp objects, burrs, thorns, seeds, or splinters in the pads or between the toes. If you find anything, remove it gently with a pair of tweezers. Also watch for soreness or blisters. If your puppy shows any signs of soreness or favors one leg, go to the veterinarian immediately.

Keep the hair on your dog's feet trimmed, because it often hides dirt, fleas, and mites. Use your blunt-nosed scissors to carefully trim the hair as close to the pads as possible. It will also give your dog a cleaner, neater appearance, especially if he has a medium or long coat.

Nail trimming is something that your dog should get used to during puppyhood. The earlier your puppy gets used to nail trimming, the easier and more relaxed grooming time will be for the both of you. Nail trimming is not only for appearances, but it is necessary for your puppy's health and comfort. It can be very difficult to get your puppy to sit still for this, which is why it is recommended to start while he is young. Also, if your puppy has a scary or painful experience, you may not get a second chance, so try to make this procedure as comfortable and routine as possible.

Avoid the quick when trimming your dog's nails.

Trimming your puppy's nails is not as hard as it may seem. The easiest way to do it is with a pair of canine nail clippers. You can also use an electric nail grinder if you find this method easier. Take care to avoid the quick, which is the area of the nail that contains nerves and blood vessels. If you accidentally cut the quick, it will bleed and be painful for your dog.

If your dog has clear or white nails, it is fairly easy to see the quick, which looks like a pink line that extends from the base of the nail toward the tip. If your dog has dark or black nails, it is harder to see where the quick ends.

The best way to trim your puppy's nails is to be conservative and only snip a tiny amount at a time. If you do cut the quick, have a styptic pencil or powder on hand to curb the bleeding.

If it makes you too nervous to trim your puppy's nails—don't ignore the task. Go to an experienced groomer. But if you start now and add it to your weekly schedule, you and your puppy will be nail-trimming experts in no time.

Ear Care

Do not neglect your puppy's ears when you groom him. Ear infections can be caused by excessive dirt, moisture, and bacteria that accumulate in the ear canal. Dogs with long, floppy ears, like some hounds, retrievers, and spaniels, are especially prone to ear problems because their ear shape prevents good air circulation. Also, dogs who often swim in natural water like lakes or rivers can get bacteria caught in their ears, causing an infection. You must be extremely diligent about keeping ears clean if you have this type of puppy.

Some breeds, like Shih Tzu, Poodles, and Lhasa Apsos, accumulate hair in the ear canal, which can trap dampness and cause infection as well. When taking care of your

Ear cleaning is an essential grooming procedure.

Gently wipe the inside of the earflap to keep ears clean.

puppy's ears, the first thing you should do is pluck or trim (with blunt-nosed scissors) the excess hair. To keep them clean, use a cotton ball or washcloth dampened with commercial ear cleaner or mineral oil, and wipe the inside of the earflap. If the ear is sore, has excess wax, or has a bad smell, your pup probably has an ear infection and needs to see the veterinarian immediately.

Ear Cleaning

Never stick anything into your puppy's ear canal. When cleaning, wipe the outside area of the earflap only, or you may damage his eardrum.

Eye Care

It is fairly easy to keep your puppy's eyes clear, sparkling, and bright. First, make sure that you keep all debris, including hair, out of the eyes. If you have a breed with a lot of facial hair, like an Old English Sheepdog, Shih Tzu, or Yorkshire Terrier, tie the hair on the top of the head with a rubber band or clip, or if you do not plan to show your dog, keep it trimmed. Wipe your dog's eyes on a regular basis with a cotton ball or washcloth dipped in warm water. If you have a breed with a lot of facial skin folds, like a Bulldog or a Chinese Shar-Pei, be sure to clean within the folds as well. If your puppy's eyes appear red, cloudy, swollen, or have excess tearing, contact your veterinarian.

Dental Care

If you do not brush your dog's teeth on a regular basis, plaque builds up on the teeth and under the gums. If this plaque is not removed, periodontal disease, which is a bacterial infection, can occur. If left untreated, the bacteria can enter the bloodstream and spread to your puppy's vital organs.

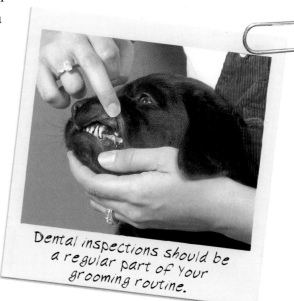

Dental inspections should be a regular part of your grooming routine.

Eating Paste

Never use human toothpaste when brushing your puppy's teeth. Dogs will not spit out the toothpaste like humans do, but will swallow it. This can cause stomach upset and other digestive problems. Also, the minty taste that humans enjoy probably will not be as appealing to your puppy as it is to you. Canine toothpaste comes in "doggy-friendly" flavors, such as beef and poultry, which are edible.

Problems, such as mouth abscesses and tooth loss, can develop as well. Puppies who don't receive good dental care can suffer from really bad breath, a feature that does not endear them to humans.

It is much easier to brush your puppy's teeth than you may think, as long as you have the right supplies. You should purchase a dog toothbrush or a finger toothbrush (a rubber cap that fits over your index finger) and toothpaste made for dogs. Start by getting your puppy used to having your fingers in his mouth. When you are performing the daily once-over, be sure to look in the pup's mouth and lift the lips or flews to expose the gums. Touch the teeth. Soon this will become just another part of your grooming routine. Then put some doggy-flavored toothpaste on the toothbrush and gently rub a few teeth at a time. Be sure to brush the teeth at the gum line.

Use a circular motion when brushing and slowly make your way around your dog's upper teeth. Make sure to get the teeth in the back of the mouth, because these are the ones most prone to periodontal disease. When you are finished with the top, do the bottom in the same manner. Daily brushing would be ideal, but try to do it at least four times a week. This will keep your dog's teeth healthy for a long time.

Part Three
Training

Rex ran off to join the circus, but he was an old dog,
and the act was looking for new tricks

Housetraining Your Puppy

When you first bring your dog home, you will probably be given plenty of advice from friends and neighbors who own dogs. You will also undoubtedly read lots of articles and books on how to raise and train your dog. No matter what anyone tells you, there is really no one training method that is superior to all others–as there is no one dog who is exactly like another. Each puppy is an individual and will respond to different techniques.

However, a dog never becomes disobedient, unruly, or a menace to society without the full

Each puppy will respond to different housetraining techniques.

There is no breed of dog that cannot be housetrained.

Hurry Up!

There's nothing worse than taking your dog for a walk on a cold, rainy day and waiting a long time for him to eliminate. Most puppies have a bad habit of thinking it's time to play when they get outside, and they forget about going to the bathroom. If you start the housetraining process early enough, you can teach your puppy to potty on command. When you take him outside, use a command for eliminating, such as "potty time," "hurry up," or "do your business." Use any command you are comfortable with and use it every time that you take your puppy to the bathroom spot. Soon, he will learn the command and go when you say it.

consent of his owner. Through heredity, genetics, or environment, your puppy may have certain limitations, but in most instances, the single biggest limitation is the owner's inability to understand the dog's needs and how to cope with them.

There is no breed that cannot be trained. Granted, there are some dogs who provide their owners with real challenges, but in most cases, these problems have more to do with the trainer than the dog. It is often simply a matter of taking the time to find out what truly motivates your puppy. Once you find a motivator, your dog will be more than willing to learn. In order to develop your puppy's potential, you should begin training the moment you bring him home.

Your eight- to ten-week-old puppy is not too young to learn; in fact, this knowledge will help your dog better deal with his new surroundings. After leaving the comfort of their mother and littermates, puppies will be insecure and look for a leader to follow. You are the one! When you establish rules from the start, you can prevent bad habits that you'll only end up correcting later.

Potty Training

One of the first things that you will undertake after acquiring your puppy will be potty training him. You are teaching your dog that there is a specific place to eliminate, preferably outside.

Household Rules

When establishing household rules, picture your pup as an adult. It may be cute to let your cuddly Saint Bernard puppy sit on your lap while you watch TV, but are you going to want a 150-pound lap dog a year from now? It may be hilarious to watch your little Chihuahua valiantly defend toys by growling at you, but in a few months the growling may turn into snapping if you don't curb this aggressiveness. Take a practical look at your life, your puppy, and your environment, and decide what behavior you can and cannot live with. It is important to make this decision now, early in your puppy's life, rather than later, because what your dog learns as a pup, he will continue doing as an adult.

The crate is a vital housetraining tool.

Your best bet is to start potty training, or housetraining, as soon as possible. However, you need to remember that puppies between the ages of 8 and 16 weeks will not have control of their bladders or bowels. They will not be able to "hold it" until they get a little older, which means that in the beginning, housetraining will take vigilance on your part. Puppies usually have to go to the bathroom after eating, drinking, sleeping, and playing. You will have to watch very carefully for signs that your puppy needs to eliminate, like circling or sniffing the floor. These behaviors are a sure sign that your puppy needs to go outside. When you see them, don't hesitate to carry your pup outside to the spot you have chosen for his elimination. Give lots of praise when he goes potty in the right place.

Crate Adventures

Some people feel that it is cruel to confine a puppy to a crate and see it as a little "puppy prison." Crates can be misused. They are not a means of ignoring your pup, nor are they meant to become a place of isolation or loneliness. Your puppy should not spend more than four hours at a time in a crate (especially when young) and should always be given plenty of time outside and with family.

A regular schedule will help you predict when your puppy needs to eliminate.

With the help of a regular schedule, you will be able to predict the times that your puppy will need to potty. The most useful thing that you can buy for him is a crate. Training your puppy to use the crate is the quickest and easiest way to housetrain him. Remember that your puppy will be developing habits that will last a lifetime—make sure that you teach him the right ones.

Crate Training

By about five weeks of age, most puppies are starting to move away from their mom and littermates to relieve themselves. This instinct to keep the bed clean is the basis of crate training. Crates work well because puppies don't want to soil where they eat and sleep. They also like to curl up in small dark places that offer protection on three sides, because it makes them feel more secure.

When you provide your puppy with a crate, you are giving your dog his very own "den." To your puppy's inner wolf, it is home sweet home. Pups will do their best to eliminate away from their dens, and later, away from your house.

Being confined in the crate will help a puppy develop better bowel and bladder control. When confined for gradually lengthened periods of time, the dog will learn to avoid soiling his bed. It is your responsibility to give your pup plenty of time outside the crate and the house, or the training process will not be successful.

Introducing the Crate

Introduce your puppy to the crate very gradually. You want the pup to feel like this is a pleasant place to be. Begin by opening the door and throwing one of your puppy's favorite treats inside. You may want to teach a command, like "bedtime" or "crate" when he goes in for the treat. Let your dog take time to investigate the crate and come and go freely, and don't forget lots of praise. Next, offer a meal in the crate. Put the food dish inside, and after a while, close the door. Open the door when your pup's done eating. Keep this up until he eats all of his meals in the crate.

Soon your puppy will be accustomed to going in and out of the crate for treats and meals. If you do not wish to continue feeding him in the crate, you can start feeding elsewhere, but continue offering a treat for going into the crate. Start closing the door and leaving the dog inside for a few minutes at a time. Gradually increase the amount of time the pup spends in the crate. Always make sure that you offer a treat and praise for going in. It is also a good idea to keep a few favorite toys inside the crate as well.

Crate Don'ts

Don't let your puppy out of the crate when crying or scratching at the door. If you do, the dog will think that complaining will bring release every time. The best thing to do for a temper tantrum is to ignore the pup. Only open the door when the pup is quiet and has calmed down.

Don't use the crate as punishment. If you use the crate when your dog does something bad, he will think of the crate as a bad place. Even if you want to get your dog out of the way, make sure that you offer lots of praise for going into the crate and give him a treat or toy, too.

Praise your puppy when he eliminates in the right place.

Part 3

Time-Out

Sometimes puppies really just need to get away from it all. The hustle and bustle of a busy household can be overwhelming at times. There are times when your puppy will get overstimulated and need to take a "time-out" to calm down (especially if you have rambunctious kids around). A crate is great for all of these times, and it should be used as your puppy's place of refuge. Soon the puppy will think it is pretty cool, too.

Your puppy will eventually become accustomed to his crate.

Crate Location

During the day, keep your puppy's crate in a location that allows easy access and permits him to be part of the family. The laundry room or backyard will make a dog feel isolated and unhappy, especially if he can hear people walking around. Place it anywhere the family usually congregates—the kitchen or family room is often the best.

At night, especially when your puppy is still getting used to the crate, the ideal place is in your bedroom, near your bed. Having you nearby will create a feeling of security and will be easier for you as well. If your dog needs to go outside during the night, you can let him out before he has an accident. Your dog will also be comforted by the smell, sight, and sound of you and will be less likely to feel frightened.

Outside Schedule

As mentioned before, puppies need time to develop bowel and bladder control. The best way to most accurately predict when your puppy needs to eliminate is to establish a routine that works well for both of you and stick to it. If you make a daily schedule of eating, drinking, and outside time and follow it, you will see your puppy progress.

Every person and family will have a different routine—there is no one right schedule for everyone. Just make sure that you arrange times and duties that everyone can stick with. The

Key to Success

A regular feeding schedule is a key factor in housetraining your puppy. If you feed your puppy at the same times every day, you'll be able to create an "outside" schedule. You will also be better able to tell how much your puppy is eating and if any problems arise.

If you can't supervise your dog, a crate might be the best option.

schedule you set up will have to work with your normal routine and lifestyle. Your first priority in the morning will be to get the puppy outdoors. Just how early this will take place will depend much more on your puppy than on you. Once your puppy comes to expect a morning walk, there will be no doubt in your mind when he needs to go out. You will also very quickly learn to tell a puppy's "emergency" signals. Do not test the young puppy's ability for self-control. A vocal demand to be let out is confirmation that the housetraining lesson is learned.

Puppies usually learn very quickly how to get your attention to go out. Unfortunately, they may learn some bad habits in the process–like barking, whining, jumping on you, or scratching at your door. You can redirect this behavior and teach your puppy a positive way to get your attention, such as ringing a bell to go outside. Hang a cowbell on the back door and smear it with some kind of treat–a little cheese works well. Each time you take your puppy outside to potty, have him reach up to lick off the cheese, thereby ringing the bell. Also ring the bell every time you let your puppy out. The action of going out is now associated with the sound of the bell and the treat. After a few months, your dog should get the picture and start ringing the bell to go outside.

Part 3

Many regular housetraining schedules can be successful.

Sticking to It

When housetraining your puppy, don't let success go to your head. A few weeks without a mistake does not mean that your puppy is completely housetrained, but it does mean your routine is working. Stick to the schedule for as long as possible. A regular schedule will be helpful now and throughout your dog's lifetime.

It is also important to limit your puppy's freedom inside the house and keep a watchful eye on him at all times. Many puppies won't take the time to go outside to relieve themselves because they are afraid they will miss something; after all, everything exciting happens in the house. That's where all the family members usually are. Unfortunately, you may find your puppy sneaking off somewhere–behind the sofa or to another room–to relieve himself. By limiting the puppy's freedom, you can prevent some of these mistakes. Close bedroom doors and put baby gates across hallways. If you can't supervise the pup, consider the crate.

One way to constantly supervise your puppy is to use what some trainers call the puppy umbilical cord. Start by attaching one end of a long leash to your puppy's collar and the other end to you. Now everywhere that you go, your dog goes, and vice versa. This method will help prevent accidents because you'll be much quicker to notice any signs that your puppy has to go outside.

The following is an example of a schedule that might work for you and your family, although remember that any schedule can work as long as you can give your dog the necessary attention.

7:00 am–Take the puppy outside. (This time might be even earlier for young puppies who have a hard time holding it all night.) After the puppy goes potty, give him lots of praise and bring him back inside. Fix the puppy's breakfast, offer water, and then take him out in the backyard.

8:00 am–Go outside to play with the puppy for a few minutes before leaving for the day. Just before you leave, put him inside the crate and give him a treat and a toy.

12:00 pm–If at all possible, come home for lunch, let your puppy out of the crate, and bring him outside to eliminate. If you or another family member can't do it, try to find a neighbor (a retired person or stay-at-home mom might be a good idea) to come over. Take this time to exercise and play with your puppy.

3:00 pm–If you have school-age children, make sure one of them comes straight home from school to take the puppy outside, walk, and play with him for a while. After playing, let the puppy hang out while your child does homework or watches television. If you do not have kids, you may be able to pay a teenager in your neighborhood to come over after school.

6:00 pm–If you are just arriving home and your dog has been confined for a few hours, immediately let him outside to eliminate and play. Feed the puppy after you eat dinner and take him outside to potty.

8:00 pm–After some quality family time, puppy included, do a little bit of grooming, offer some water, and then take the pup outside to eliminate.

11:00 pm–Take the puppy outside one last time before going to bed.

Keep in mind that he should not remain in the crate for longer than three to four hours at a time, except during the night. In addition, the puppy will need to go out after waking up, eating, playtime, and every three to four hours in between.

Oops!

If your puppy does eliminate in your house, make sure you clean it up right away with a pet-odor neutralizer, which can be bought in a pet store. This should keep him from using the same spot again. You can also scrub the area thoroughly with a solution of 1/4 cup of white vinegar and a squirt of liquid detergent mixed with 1 quart of warm water.

Part 3

Accidents Will Happen

When housetraining your dog, remember that if the puppy has an accident, it means that he was not supervised well enough or wasn't taken outside in time. If you catch your dog in the act, don't yell or scold him. Simply say, "No!" loudly, which should startle and stop the dog. Pick him up and go outside so he can continue eliminating in the regular relief area. Praise the pup for finishing outside. If you scold or punish him, you are teaching him that you think going potty is wrong. Your dog will become sneaky about it, and you will find puddles and piles in strange places. Don't concentrate on correction; emphasize the praise for eliminating in the right place.

A housetraining accident means that your dog wasn't supervised well enough.

Housetraining is one of the most important gifts we can give our dogs. It allows them to live as one of the family. Every puppy will make mistakes, especially in the beginning. Do not worry—with the proper training and lots of patience, every dog can be housetrained.

Part 3

13

Basic Training for Good Behavior

The Right to Be Trained

All puppies not only need basic training–they deserve it. Dogs do not automatically know how they should behave, so they need rules to follow. Puppies' rights include having the basic tools in order to fit in with the new family. Once dogs know these things, they are usually perfectly willing to do whatever is necessary in order to fit in with the family pack. When you provide this opportunity, you are ensuring that you and your puppy will get along beautifully for the duration of your life together.

All puppies will benefit from basic training.

Treats are a positive training reinforcer.

Why Is Training Important?

When you added a puppy to your family, you probably wanted a companion and a friend. You may have wanted a dog to accompany you on walks, jog alongside you, or play with your children. Perhaps you wanted to get involved in dog sports or events. To do any of these things, your puppy will need training.

Training is important, because it will transform your jumpy, squirmy, wiggly little puppy into a well-mannered dog who is a joy to be around. A trained puppy won't jump up on people, dash out the door, or raid the trashcan.

All puppies need to have someone tell them what to do. Puppies have the right to be trained–it is unfair to expect them to figure out the human world on their own, and they won't be able to do it.

You, too, will benefit from training, because you will learn how to motivate your puppy, how to prevent problem behaviors, and how to correct mistakes that do happen. Puppy training entails much more than the traditional sit, down, stay, and come commands–it means that you will be teaching your puppy how to live in your house. You can set some rules and expect him to follow them.

First, you must decide exactly what you want training to accomplish. You probably want your puppy to be calm and well behaved around people and well mannered when out in public. Maybe you would like to participate in dog activities and sports. The things that you can do with your puppy are unlimited. Decide what you would like to do and then embark on a training program to achieve those goals.

Part 3

Professional Training

When it comes to training your puppy, one option is to find a trainer to help you out. If you decide to take your puppy to a training class, you must do your homework. It should be your mission to find the trainer in your area that would be best for both you and your puppy.

Training Methods

Obedience instructors teach a dog owner how to train his or her own dog. There are thousands of dog trainers, and each one will have a method or technique based on his or her personality, teaching techniques, experience, and philosophy regarding dogs and dog training. Any given method may work wonderfully for one dog but fail for another.

Because there are so many different techniques, styles, and methods, choosing a particular instructor may be difficult. It is important to understand various methods so that you can make a reasonable decision.

Compulsive Training

Compulsive training is a correction-based training style that sometimes uses forceful corrections in order to shape behavior. It is often used in conjunction with law enforcement. It is rarely the

A professional trainer might be the best option for you and your dog.

Every instructor has a different style of training.

right type of training technique for a puppy, and many dog owners do not like compulsive training because they feel that it can be too rough.

Inducive Training

Inducive training is exactly the opposite of compulsive training. Instead of being forced to do something, the dog is induced or motivated toward proper behavior. Depending on the instructor, there are few or no corrections used. Inducive training works very well for most puppies, non-aggressive dogs, and owners who dislike corrections.

Most trainers use a combination of compulsive and inducive training.

Questions to Ask the Trainer

Once you have a list of referrals for dog trainers in your area, call the instructors and ask questions such as:

✓ How long have you been teaching classes?

✓ What do you think of my breed?

✓ What training methods do you use?

✓ Do you belong to any professional organizations?

✓ Can I observe your classes? There should be no reason why you cannot attend a class to observe the instructor. (If you can't watch, cross this one off your list.)

When you go to watch the class, ask yourself these questions:

✓ Would you let this person handle your dog?

✓ How does the instructor relate to the dogs?

✓ Are the dogs relaxed and looking like they're having a good time?

✓ Are the dogs paying attention to the instructor?

If you're still not sure, don't be afraid to keep asking questions. You are paying a trainer to provide a service, and you must be sure that both you and your puppy will be comfortable with your decision.

Part 3

Unfortunately, inducive training is not always the right technique for all puppies, because intelligent dogs who have dominant personalities may take advantage of the lack of corrections or discipline. They will then set their own rules, which may not be agreeable to their owners.

The Middle Road

The majority of trainers and instructors use a method that is somewhere between compulsive training and inducive training. An inducive method is used when possible, and corrections are used when needed. Obviously, the range can be vast, with some trainers leaning more toward corrections and others using as few as possible.

Finding an Instructor or Trainer

Referrals are probably the best place to start when trying to find an instructor or trainer. If you have admired a neighbor's well-behaved puppy, ask where he or she went for training. Call your veterinarian, breeder, or groomer and ask who they recommend. Make notes about each referral. What did people like and dislike about this trainer? You will want an experienced trainer who can handle any situation that may arise. However, experience is not the only qualification. Some people who have been training dogs for years are still using the same teaching method and haven't learned any new techniques. Ideally, the trainer you choose should be knowledgeable about your dog's breed characteristics, personality, and temperament and know how to train him. If he or she doesn't like the breed, go elsewhere.

A good training instructor will belong to a professional training organization. The National Association of Dog Obedience Instructors (NADOI) and the Association of Pet Dog Trainers (APDT) are two of the more prominent groups. Both of these organizations publish regular newsletters to share information, techniques, and new developments with their members. Instructors who belong to these organizations are more likely to be up-to-date on training techniques and styles, as well as information about specific dog breeds.

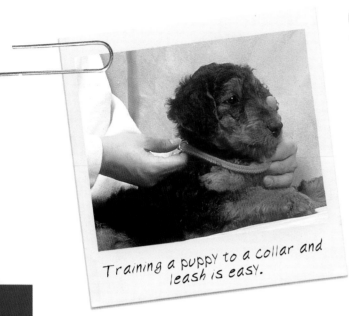

Training a puppy to a collar and leash is easy.

To Pull or Not to Pull

If your puppy is nervous on the leash, never pull him to your side as you may see so many other people do. The pup must always come to you voluntarily. When the dog sees you yanking on the leash, he knows that you are the one doing the correcting. When racing ahead, your pup does not see you jerk the leash and only knows that something is restricting his movement. Once back in position, give lots of praise, which is using canine psychology to your advantage.

Collar and Leash Training

Training a puppy to a collar and leash is easy and something you can start doing at home without assistance. Start with a soft nylon collar. The puppy will initially try to bite at it but will soon forget it's there, more so if you play with him. Some people leave the dog's collar on all of the time, while others put it on only when they are taking the dog out. If it is to be left on, purchase a narrow or round one so it does not mark the coat or become snagged on furniture.

Once the puppy ignores the collar, you can attach the leash to it and let him pull it behind him for a few minutes every day. However, if the pup starts to chew at the leash, simply keep it slack and let him choose where to go. The idea is to let your pup get the feel of the leash but not get in the habit of chewing it. Repeat this a couple of times a day for two days, and the pup will get used to the leash without feeling restrained.

Now, you can let the pup understand that the leash will be restrictive. The first time this happens, your dog will either pull, buck, or just sit down. Immediately call the pup to you and give lots of praise. Never tug on the leash or drag the puppy along the floor. This might cause him to associate the leash with negative consequences. After a few lessons, the puppy will be familiar with the restrictive feeling, and you can start going in the opposite direction from him. Give the leash a short tug so that the pup is brought to a halt, call him to you enthusiastically, and continue walking. When the puppy is walking happily on the leash, end the lesson with lots of praise. There is no rush for your puppy to learn leash training, so take as long as you need to make him feel comfortable.

Puppy Kindergarten

The next step in training should be a class that is geared just for puppies. Puppy kindergarten classes consist of obedience training and socialization and are for puppies between the ages of 10 and 16 weeks. A puppy owner also learns how to prevent problem behaviors from occurring and how to establish household rules.

Your dog will gradually become used to the feel of his leash.

Every puppy can benefit from this type of class. It will teach the foundations of training, as well as provide an excellent opportunity for socialization with other dogs and people. A good puppy kindergarten class will teach you how to train and teach your dog obedience commands, like come, sit, stay, down, and heel. Participating in a kindergarten class with your puppy will strengthen the bond between you, bring you closer together, and help you to learn the right way to train your dog. After your puppy passes puppy kindergarten, the sky's the limit!

Basic Commands

Although your puppy should attend puppy kindergarten, begin training as soon as he is comfortable in your home and knows his name. It is also very helpful to take the lessons that you learn together in kindergarten and practice them at home. Doing your

Part 3

Keep water on hand for outdoor training sessions.

Part 3

Begin training as soon as your puppy is comfortable with you and knows his name.

"homework" together will not only reinforce what you learn in class, it will allow you to spend some quality one-on-one time with your pup.

There are two very important things to remember when training your puppy: Train the puppy without any potential distractions and keep all lessons very short. Eliminating any distraction is important because it is essential that you have your pup's full attention. This is not possible if there are other people, other dogs, butterflies, or birds to play with. Also, always remember that puppies have very short attention spans. Even when the pup has become a young adult, the maximum time you should train would be about 20 minutes. However, you can give the puppy more than one lesson a day, three being as many as recommended, each spaced well apart. If you train any longer, the puppy will become bored, and you will end the session on a down note, which you should never do.

Before beginning a lesson, always play a little game so that the puppy is in an active state of mind and more receptive to training. Likewise, always end lessons with play and on a high note, lavishly praising the puppy, which will build his confidence.

The Come Command

The come command is possibly the most important one you can teach–it may even save your pup's life someday. It ensures that your dog will return to you immediately when you call, even if there is any kind of distraction or danger nearby. Teaching your puppy to come when called should always be a pleasant experience. You should never call your puppy in order to scold or yell at him, or he will soon learn not to respond. When your pup comes to you, make sure to give lots of praise, petting, and in the beginning, a treat. If your dog expects happy things when reaching your side, you'll never have trouble getting him to come to you.

Start with your puppy on a long lead (about 20 feet in length) and have plenty of treats that he likes. Walk the distance of the lead, then crouch down and say, "Come." Make sure that you use a happy, excited tone of voice with the pup's name. Your puppy should come to you enthusiastically. If not, use the long lead to pull him toward you, but continue to use that happy tone of voice. Your puppy should learn from the start that not coming when called is not an option. Give lots of praise and a treat when your pup gets there. Continue to use the long lead until he is consistently obeying your command.

Training should take place without any outside distractions.

The Sit Command

As with most basic commands, your puppy will learn this one in just a few lessons. One 15-minute lesson each day should do the trick in no time. Some trainers will advise you not to proceed to other commands until the previous one has been

Hand Signals

People usually think that obeying hand signals is something that only dogs with advanced training can do. Actually, you can start teaching your puppy hand signals from the very beginning. Ask your trainer to help you incorporate the hand signals as you learn the commands and use them in your everyday practice. They can be very useful, especially when your dog is at a distance from you.

Part 3

Just to Be Near You

Puppyhood is the easiest time to teach the come command, because most puppies want to be near you anyway. Take advantage of this natural reaction and start teaching the come command as soon as you get your puppy home. Whenever he decides to run to you, just give the come command. The dog will learn to associate the action with the words, and it will reinforce your position as the pack leader.

The sit can be learned in just a few lessons.

learned really well. However, a bright young pup is quite capable of handling more than one command per lesson or certainly per day. As time progresses, you will be going through each command as a matter of routine before a new one is attempted. This is so the puppy always starts as well as ends a lesson on a high note, having successfully completed a task.

There are two ways to teach the sit command. First, get a treat that your dog really likes and hold it right by his nose, so that all attention is focused on it. Raise the treat above his head and say, "Sit." Usually, the puppy will follow the treat and automatically sit. Give him the treat for being such a good dog, and don't forget to praise him. After a while, the pup will begin to associate the word "sit" with the action. Most puppies will catch on very quickly. Once your dog is sitting reliably with the treat, take it away and just use praise as a reward.

However, there are some puppies that are more stubborn than others, and they may need a little more encouragement to get the picture. If your puppy doesn't sit automatically when the treat is overhead, place one hand on his hindquarters and the other under the upper chest. Say, "Sit" in a pleasant (never harsh) voice. At the same time, lightly push down on his rear and push up under the chest until he is sitting. Now give lots of praise and a treat. Repeat this a few times and your pet will get the idea. Most puppies will also tend to stand up at first, so immediately repeat the exercise.

Confusion in the Ranks

Don't confuse your puppy by using the down command for anything other than lying down. For example, if you want the dog to get off the couch, use another word, like "off," to get your point across. This way, when you teach the down command, there will be no doubt in your dog's mind what you expect.

Use treats to teach your puppy to sit.

When the puppy understands the command and does it right away, you can slowly move backward so that you are a few feet away. If the dog attempts to come to you, simply go back to the original position and start again. Do not attempt to keep the pup in the sit position for too long. Even a few seconds is a long time for an impatient, energetic puppy, and you do not want your dog to get bored with lessons even before beginning them.

The Stay Command

This command should follow the sit, but it can be very hard for puppies to understand. Remember that your puppy wants nothing more than to be at your side, so it will be hard for a dog to stay in one place while you walk away. You should only expect your pup to perform this command for a few seconds at first, and gradually work up to longer periods of time.

Face the puppy and say, "Sit." Now step backward, saying, "Stay." It is also very helpful to use a hand signal for stay–place your hand straight out, palm toward the dog's nose.

Part 3

Let the pup remain in the position for only a few seconds before saying, "Come," and giving lots of praise and a treat. Once your dog gets the hang of it, repeat the command again, but step farther back. If the pup gets up and comes to you, simply go back to the original position and start again. As the pup starts to understand the command, you can move farther and farther back.

Once your puppy is staying reliably from a short distance, the next test is to walk away after placing the pup. This will mean that your back is to the dog, which will tempt him to follow you. Keep an eye over your shoulder, and the minute the pup starts to move, spin around, say, "Stay," and start over from the original position.

As the weeks go by, you can increase the length of time the pup is left in the stay position–but two to three minutes is quite long enough for a puppy. If your puppy drops into a down position and is clearly more comfortable, there is nothing wrong with it. In the beginning, staying put is good enough!

The Down Command

From the puppy's viewpoint, the down command is one of the most difficult to accept. This position is submissive in a wild pack situation. A timid dog will roll over, which is a natural gesture of submission. A bolder pup will want to get up and might back off, not wanting to submit. The dog will feel as though

Once your dog is performing reliably, use praise as a training reward.

Roll Over

A fun trick to teach after your puppy masters the down is the roll over. Once your dog is in the down position, hold a treat in front of him. When he is focused, bring the treat back and gently help him to roll over on to his stomach, saying, "Roll over" as you do it. Complete the circle with the treat in your hands until your dog is back in the down position. It may take some coaxing and a little help at first, but your puppy should be rolling over in no time.

he's about to be punished, which would be the position in a natural environment. Once the pup understands this is not the case and that there are rewards for obeying, he will accept this position without any problem.

You may notice that some dogs will sit very quickly but will respond to the down command more slowly. It is their way of saying that they will obey the command, but under protest!

There are two ways to teach the down command. Obviously, with a puppy, it will be easier to teach the down if you are kneeling next to your dog. With dogs who are willing to please, the following method should work: Have your dog sit and hold a treat in front of his nose. When his full attention is on the treat, start to lower the treat slowly to the ground, saying, "Down." The dog should follow the treat with his head. Bring the treat out slowly in front of the pup. If you are really lucky, your puppy's legs will slide forward and he will lie down. Give him the treat and lots of praise for being such a good dog. For a dog who won't lie down on his own (and most puppies won't), you can try this method: After the puppy is sitting and focused on the treat, take his front legs and gently sweep them forward, at the same time saying, "Down." Release the legs and quickly apply light

End on a High Note!

After a while, you should be able to move from one command to the next with no problem. If you run into a problem, it is probably because the puppy does not understand the command thoroughly, the training sessions are too long, or he is bored. Sometimes, the dog may just be having a bad day. If he just doesn't seem to be into the training session, do a simple exercise your dog knows well and call it a day. Be sure to use praise and play so that you end on a note of accomplishment.

When your dog is familiar with sit and stay, begin teaching the down.

Part 3

pressure on the shoulders with your left hand. Then tell the dog how good he is, give the treat, and make a lot of fuss. Repeat two or three times only in one training session. The pup will learn over a few lessons. Remember that this is a very submissive act on the pup's behalf, so there is no need to rush matters.

The Heel Command

All dogs should be able to walk nicely on a leash without a tug-of-war with their owners. Teaching your puppy the heel command should follow leash training. Heeling is best done in a place where you have a wall or a fence to one side of you, because it will restrict the puppy's movements so that you only have to contend with forward and backward situations. Again, it is better to do the lesson in private and not in a place where there will be many distractions.

There will probably be no need to use a slip collar on your puppy, as you can be just as effective with a flat, buckle one. The leash should be approximately 6 feet long. You can adjust the space between you, the puppy, and the wall so that your pet has only a small amount of room to move sideways. It is also very helpful to have a treat in your hand so that your dog will be focused on you and stay by your side.

Hold the leash in your right hand and pass it through to your left. As the puppy moves

Bad Dog or Bad Health?

If your dog displays behavior problems, it may not be because of lack of training. Some experts feel that 20 percent of all behavior problems are health-related. Housetraining accidents could be caused by bladder infections or gastrointestinal upset, and medical problems like thyroid imbalance can cause hyperactivity. Poor nutrition can also be a factor. Chewing on garden plants or wood could indicate that your puppy is not getting enough nutrients, and food allergies are often the cause of behavior problems. Before you start training your dog, make sure he has been to the veterinarian and has received a clean bill of health. Once health problems have been ruled out, you can start correcting any unwanted behavior.

ahead, pull on the leash and give a quick jerk backward with your left hand, while at the same time saying, "Heel." You want the pup's head to be at, but not touching, your knee. When the puppy is in this position, praise him and begin walking again. Repeat the whole exercise. Once the puppy begins to get the message, then you can use your left hand (with the treat inside of it) to pat the side of your knee so that the pup is encouraged to keep close to your side.

Keeping your dog on leash will ensure his safety while on walks.

When the pup understands the basics, you can mix up the lesson a little to keep him focused. Do an about-turn, or make a quick left or right, which will result in a sudden jerk as you move in the opposite direction. The puppy will now be behind you, so you can pat your knee and say, "Heel." As soon as the pup is in the correct position, give lots of praise. The puppy will now begin to associate certain words with certain actions. When not in the heel position, your dog will experience discomfort as you jerk the leash. When the pup is alongside of you, he will receive praise. Given these two options, dogs will always prefer the praise.

Once the lesson is learned and the dog is heeling reliably, then you can change your pace from a slow walk to a quick one, and the puppy will adjust. The slow walk is always the more difficult for most puppies, as they are usually anxious to be on the move. End the lesson when the pup is walking nicely beside you. Begin the lesson with a few sit commands so you're starting with success and praise.

The Recall to Heel Command

To teach this command, have the pup in front of you in the sit position with his collar and leash on. Hold the leash in your right hand. Give the command to heel and pat your left knee. As the pup starts to move forward, use your right hand to guide him

Part 3

Gradually work your way up to more extensive training sessions.

The no command could save your dog's life.

behind you. If you need to, you can hold the collar and walk the dog around your back to the desired position. You will need to repeat this a few times until the puppy understands what you want.

When you've done this a number of times, you can try it without the collar and leash. Bring the dog to a sit position in front of you, hold the collar, and walk him around the back of you. The dog will eventually understand and automatically pass around your back each time. If the dog is already behind you when you give the heel command, then the pup should automatically come to your left side. If necessary, pat your left leg.

The No Command

This is a command that must be obeyed every time; your puppy must understand it 100 percent. Most delinquent dogs–the jumpers, the barkers, and the biters–have never been taught this command. If your puppy were to approach any potential danger, the no command, coupled with the come command, could be a lifesaver.

You do not need a specific lesson for this command; it will most likely be used every day. You must be consistent and apply it every time your dog does something wrong. It is best, however, to be able to replace the negative command with something positive. This way, your puppy will respond quicker. For example, if your puppy is chewing on your shoe, say, "No!" and replace the shoe with a toy. Then heap on the praise.

Part 3

Problem Solving

Dogs will be dogs. Behaviors that we may consider to be "problems" are often just puppies doing what puppies do. Things like barking, digging, and jumping up are natural puppy instincts. You must teach him what behavior you want in your home–the dog will not know automatically.

Basic obedience training is the first step toward controlling problem behavior. All training should reinforce your role as leader in the family pack and that your dog has to obey your rules. Basic training should also reinforce the fact that you are a reasonable and kind leader and that by obeying you, your puppy will reap all sorts of benefits and rewards. Once your puppy knows these things, it should be fairly easy to control his behavior.

Remember that puppies have a seemingly unlimited amount of energy and will get into mischief if this energy is not properly directed. Puppies who are bored or restless will look for things to do, such as digging up your flower beds or running out the door when it's opened. If you provide your puppy with plenty of play and exercise, he will be too tired to get into trouble.

There are some common puppy behaviors that may cause problems in your house. The good news is that with the proper training and motivation, they can be dealt with easily.

Barking

Some owners think that they want their dog to bark–that it makes the puppy a good watchdog. However, this is a habit that should not be encouraged. Most dogs will bark

Too Much Fun?

You should be particularly careful with young children, because they can unintentionally play too roughly with puppies who still have their deciduous (baby) teeth. Those teeth are like needles and can leave little scars on youngsters. Be sure to supervise playtime between your children and your puppy, and intervene with a "time-out" for both parties if the fun gets out of hand.

Shake, Shake, Shake...

Dog trainer Alexandra Allred suggests the "shake-can" method to catch the runaway puppy. First, make a shake-can—about 15 pennies in a tin bandage box will usually do the trick. Then, with the can in your hand, call your puppy's name. When the dog does not come immediately, shake the can, and at the same time, command your puppy to come to you. If there is still no response, yell, "No!" and throw the can near the dog. The idea is to throw the can beyond the puppy so that he cannot see where it lands. This way, the dog will be startled by the noise and run to the owner for protection, which of course you should offer, along with affection and praise. Allred says it never fails—in one case, the puppy would hear the can shake and run right past the owner, into the house, up the stairs, and into his crate!

anyway when a stranger comes to the door or into their territory. What you don't want is a dog who barks at every car that drives by or every leaf that falls into the yard. This is not only annoying to you but to the entire neighborhood as well.

Plenty of play and exercise will keep your puppy out of mischief.

Barking can be a problem in some breeds or a bad habit that is acquired. It takes the owner's dedication to stop his or her dog's barking. First, you should figure out the cause. Is the dog seeking attention or does he need to go out? Is it feeding time, is the dog alone, or is it a protective bark? If the barking seems to be caused by something simple, like barking to go outside or because the dog is hungry, it should be easy to control this behavior.

Overzealous barking can be an inherited tendency, but a lot of puppy barking is due to boredom. If your puppy barks for attention or when left alone, you can take steps to stop it. If you notice that your puppy barks for attention, you must not reinforce the bad behavior. Never give attention when he is barking. Wait until the dog is quiet, and then use petting and praise. If the barking starts again, walk away and ignore the pup. He should get the picture in no time. If you notice that your dog barks when left alone, there are a few things you can try. Before you leave, see that the pup has been walked, fed, and given water. Be sure to allow plenty of time for exercise before you leave–a sleeping puppy will not be a barking puppy. Make sure you curb your dog's boredom by providing him with lots of toys while you're gone. Leave a radio tuned to an easy-listening station for company. Pull the shades or close the curtains. Eventually, the dog will get used to time alone, especially if he's having fun all alone.

Jumping Up

A puppy who jumps up is a happy puppy. However, while it's cute when the dog is small, few guests appreciate dogs jumping on them, especially when your sweet little Great Dane pup continues this habit into adulthood. There will come a time, probably around four months of age, when your puppy will need to know when it is okay to jump and when good manners, such as sitting, are better.

How do you correct the problem? Teach the puppy the sit command as soon as he starts to jump up. The sit must be practiced every time your dog starts to jump up. Don't forget to give lots of praise for good behavior. Remember that the entire family must take part by reinforcing the sit. Each time you allow the dog to jump, you go back a step in training, because your puppy will not understand that it is okay to jump on some people but not others.

To discourage jumping up, encourage your dog to sit.

Misplaced Aggression

Lacy was a Sheltie who seemed afraid of everything—I mean everything! She would attack the phone every time it rang and the kitchen cabinet every time the microwave finished heating a meal. Her family thought this was hilarious behavior and would laugh and laugh—even applaud—every time she did it. To Lacy, it was clear that her family was living in terror of these irritating noises until she came along. The fact that it made her family happy when she protected them just reinforced the behavior. Then she really couldn't understand why they were so mad at her when she destroyed the telephone and ate away most of the cabinet that held the microwave. Wasn't she just getting closer to solving everyone's problems? Lacy's behavior is an example of what happens when you reinforce your puppy's aggression toward new objects or noises. If her family had ignored the behavior and redirected her to something else, like a toy or a bone, they might not be remodeling their kitchen right now.

Teach your puppy early that biting is unacceptable.

Biting

All puppies bite and try to chew on your fingers, toes, arms, etc. This is the time to teach them to be gentle and not to bite hard. First, put your fingers in your puppy's mouth and allow him to bite. If the bites are too hard, say, "Easy!" Let the pup know he's hurting you by squealing and acting like you have been seriously hurt. Do not continue to play until he has calmed down. If your dog doesn't respond to the corrections, then a "time-out" in the crate is needed.

Biting in the more mature dog is something that should be prevented at all costs. If it occurs, quickly communicate in no uncertain terms that biting will not be tolerated. A dog bite is serious and should be given immediate attention. Wash the bite with soap and water and contact your doctor. It is important to know the status of the offender's rabies vaccination.

Your dog must know who is boss. When biting occurs, you should seek professional help at once, either through your veterinarian, dog trainer, and/or behaviorist.

Digging

Bored dogs release their frustrations through mischievous behavior such as digging. Puppies shouldn't be left outside unattended for long periods of time, even if they are in a fenced-in yard. Usually the puppy is sent to the backyard because the owner cannot tolerate the dog in the house.

Dogs crave companionship and should not be left alone for long periods.

The puppy feels socially deprived and needs to be included in his owner's life. In fact, the puppy only wants to develop into the companion that his owner desired in the first place. Let your puppy in the house and allow him to participate in family activities as much as possible.

If you do need to leave your dog outside and do not want your yard to look like a mine field, the best solution is to build a dog run. Fence off a space that will be large enough for the dog to move about when he is fully grown. Provide shelter, food, and water, and keep it stocked with lots of bones and toys. This way, your puppy will get to enjoy time outside without you having to monitor his every move.

Born to Run

If dogs are never let off leash except when supervised in a fenced-in yard, they can't do much running away. However, there is always the dog who seems to have been an escape artist in another life and will get out no matter how diligent you are.

Part 3

A fenced-in yard is an important safety measure.

When you catch your runaway dog, never punish him.

Perhaps your puppy escapes while you are both playing in the yard and refuses to come when called. If your puppy is not in immediate danger, the best thing is to use a little reverse psychology. Do not chase your dog; he will just think that you are playing a game and will run farther. Use what you know, namely that your dog loves to be with you. Puppies never want to miss out on the fun. Try calling his name in a happy, excited tone of voice and then running in the opposite direction. Most likely, your curious puppy will want in on the game and start to follow you. You can then turn around and call him to you. Always kneel down when trying to catch the runaway, because dogs can be intimidated by people standing over them. It is always helpful to have a treat or a favorite toy to help entice the pup to your side.

Remember that when you finally do catch your naughty dog, you must not use discipline. After all, there could be a repeat performance, and it would be nice if next time your dog would respond to your come command.

Until the dog responds reliably to the come command every time, attach a long line to him. The puppy will not be able to judge how long the line is, and you can grab the line without getting too close or step on it to stop the dog. Then just reel in your "fish" with a big smile and lots of praise. As the dog matures and masters basic obedience, he will realize it is a pleasure to be at your side and will eagerly come every time you call.

Fear

One of the most common problems that puppies experience is fear reactions. Some dogs are more afraid than others, depending on their temperament, the socialization that they have received, and their early environment. Sometimes, dogs can be afraid of a strange object, which is sometimes humorous to watch. They act silly when something is out of place in the house. This problem is called perceptive intelligence. Dogs realize the abnormal within their known environment. They may not react the same way in strange environments, because they do not know what is normal.

A shy puppy will need time to adjust to his surroundings.

A more serious fear is a fear of people. This can result in behavior that includes backing away or hiding, or it can result in an aggressive behavior that may lead to challenging a person or fear biting. This can really be a problem if there are young, rambunctious children in the house who may unintentionally frighten or overwhelm the puppy.

Hopefully, you have chosen a puppy who has a temperament that fits in with your household. The best type of household for a pup who displays fear or timidity is one with adults who will respect the puppy's feelings. If your puppy is timid of new situations or people, respect that the dog wants to be left alone and allow time for him to come forward. If you approach, the cornered dog may resort to snapping. Left alone, the dog may decide to come out voluntarily, which should be rewarded with a treat.

Dogs can be afraid of numerous things, including loud noises and thunderstorms.

Part 3

Invariably, the owner rewards the dog's fearfulness by comforting him. Instead, direct your dog's attention to something else and act perfectly normal. For example, if your puppy is barking at the new plant in the living room, simply go up to the plant, touch it, and say something in a happy tone of voice. Don't dwell on the fright. Act normally and show him that there is nothing to be afraid of.

Aggression

Aggression is the most common behavioral problem encountered. Protective breeds can be more aggressive than others, but with the proper upbringing and training, they can make very dependable companions. Many factors contribute to aggression, including genetics and environment. An improper environment, which may include poor living conditions, lack of socialization, excessive punishment, or being attacked or frightened, can all influence a dog's behavior. Even spoiling a puppy and reinforcing aggressive behavior may be detrimental. Isolation, lack of human contact, or exposure to frequent teasing by children or adults also can ruin a good dog.

In addition, lack of direction, fear, or confusion can lead to aggression in those dogs who are so inclined. Any obedience exercises, such as the sit and the down, can redirect the puppy's attention and help him overcome any fear or confusion. When your puppy shows signs of aggression, you should speak calmly (no screaming or hysterics) and firmly give a command he understands, such as the sit. As soon as your dog obeys, you have assumed the dominant position. Some puppies show too much aggression for their owners to handle. If caution is exercised and professional help is gained early on, most cases can be controlled.

If you have done everything according to the book regarding training and socialization and are still dealing with a behavior problem, don't procrastinate. The problem needs to receive professional attention before it gets out of hand.

Separation Anxiety

Separation anxiety occurs when puppies feel distress or apprehension while separated from their owners. One mistake that owners make is to set the pups up for their departure. This will lead to barking, crying, and whining, and for puppies who are really anxious, destruction of your house a few minutes after you're gone. The bigger the fuss you make over leaving, the bigger the fuss your dog will make when you leave. Some authorities recommend paying little attention to the pet for at least ten minutes before leaving and for the first ten minutes after you arrive home. If you keep your coming and going as low key as possible, the dog won't be aware that you are leaving and will learn to accept it as a normal everyday occurrence.

Separation anxiety occurs when dogs feel distressed when separated from their owners.

Right before you leave, give your puppy something interesting to play with—perhaps one of those balls that dispenses a biscuit when it rolls around. You might also put some treats in a paper bag and tape it shut. This should keep your pet so busy that he won't even notice that you are gone. And remember, don't remind him—just go! Crate your dog or confine him to one safe room when you leave. This will keep your dog and your belongings safe.

Food Guarding

If your puppy guards his food by growling or snapping at anyone who tries to get close when he's eating, you should correct the problem

A fun toy may distract your dog and alleviate his separation anxiety.

Food guarding is a problem behavior that should be corrected immediately.

immediately. First, it is not fair to feed your puppy in a busy environment where children or other pets may interfere with his mealtime. This constant interference can be the cause of food guarding. If this is the problem in your house, feed your puppy in his crate, where he will not feel threatened. Also, instruct your children not to bother any dog who is eating.

Start by feeding the pup out of your hand, which teaches him that it is okay for you to remove a food bowl or toy, and you will return it. Make the dog work for this reward (dinner) by doing some obedience command such as sit or down before you break out the food. Do the same thing if your puppy shows possessiveness over toys. Take them away and then give them back, with lots of praise for being a good dog. This is just another instance of teaching your puppy that you are the leader of the pack. Once this is established, there should be no problems.

Submissive Urination

Submissive urination is not a housetraining problem but rather a psychological problem. It can occur in all breeds and may be more prevalent in some. Usually it occurs in puppies and may be in response to physical praise or overexcitement. Many dogs outgrow this problem, and scolding will only make the problem worse. Try verbal praise instead of physical petting for a while, and make sure that your dog has had a chance to urinate outdoors before playing with you.

Coprophagia

Also known as stool eating, coprophagia is a habit that sometimes occurs without cause. Puppies may start this because they are bored. This is a habit that is hard to break. The best remedy is to keep the puppy on a leash when out for walks. Also, keep the yard clean so that there will be no opportunity to get in trouble. If it becomes a real problem, your veterinarian can give you something to put on the puppy's food that makes the stool have a bitter taste.

The Canine Good Citizen® Test

A good way to make sure that your puppy has good manners is to train him for the Canine Good Citizen® test. The American Kennel Club (AKC) has developed this program to encourage all owners to properly train their dogs. It emphasizes responsible dog ownership and teaches your puppy good manners in the home and the community. All dogs of any age, purebred or mixed breed, can take the Canine Good Citizen® test and earn a certificate from the AKC, as well as add the CGC® title to their name.

The dog must complete ten steps in order to pass. These exercises show that the dog is a pet that any person would like to own, that he is safe with children, and that he would be welcomed as a neighbor. An increasing number of states have now passed Canine Good Citizen® legislation and the CGC® program has been adopted in several other countries.

The American Kennel Club encourages all dog owners to participate in this program, and you can find out where a test is being given in your area by contacting your local breed club or the AKC directly.

In order to earn a CGC®, your puppy must pass the following tests:

Test 1: Accepting a Friendly Stranger
This demonstrates that your dog will allow a friendly stranger to approach and speak to you in a natural, everyday situation. You and the evaluator will shake hands and exchange pleasantries. Your dog must show no shyness or sign of resentment and must not break position or approach the evaluator.

Part 3

The AKC encourages dog owners to participate in the CGC® test.

Test 2: Sitting Politely for Petting

This test demonstrates your dog's ability to let a friendly stranger touch him while he is out with you. Your dog should sit at your side as the evaluator approaches and pets the dog on the head or body only. Your dog may stand in place to accept petting and must not show any shyness or resentment.

Test 3: Appearance and Grooming

This practical test demonstrates that your dog will welcome being groomed and examined and will permit a stranger, such as a veterinarian, groomer, or friend of yours, to do so also. It also demonstrates your level of care, concern, and sense of responsibility. The evaluator inspects your dog and combs or brushes him, then lightly examines the ears and each front foot.

Test 4: Walking on a Loose Leash

This test demonstrates that you are in control of the dog. Your dog may be on either side of the handler, whichever you prefer. There must be a left turn, a right turn, and an about turn, with at least one stop in between and another at the end. Your dog does not have to be perfectly aligned with you and does not need to sit when you stop.

Test 5: Walking Through a Crowd

This test demonstrates that your dog can move about politely in pedestrian traffic and is under control in public places. You and your dog will walk around and pass close to several people (at least three). Your dog may show some interest in the strangers without appearing overexuberant, shy, or resentful. You may talk to the dog and use encouragement or praise throughout the test. Your dog should not be straining on the leash.

Test 6: Sit and Down on Command/Staying in Place

This demonstrates that your dog has had training, will respond to your sit and down commands, and will remain in the position you command. You may choose sit or down, whichever you prefer. You may take a reasonable amount of time and use more than one command to make the dog do the sit and the down. When instructed by the evaluator, you must tell your dog to stay and walk forward the length of a 20-foot line. Your dog must remain in place but may change positions.

Test 7: Coming When Called

This test demonstrates that your dog will come when you call. You will walk 20 feet away, then turn to face the dog and call him to you. You may use encouraging words to get your dog to come to you. You may tell him to stay or wait, or you may simply walk away, giving no instructions as the evaluator provides mild distractions, such as petting, etc.

Test 8: Reaction to Another Dog

This test demonstrates that your dog can behave politely around other dogs. You and your dog will meet another handler and dog, approach each other from a distance of about 10 yards, stop, shake hands and exchange pleasantries, and continue on for about 5 more yards. The dogs should show no more than a casual interest in one another.

The CGC® test promotes responsible dog ownership.

Test 9: Reactions to Distractions

This test demonstrates that your dog is confident when faced with common distracting situations, such as the dropping of a large book or the passing of a jogger in front of the dog. Your dog may express a natural interest and

A well-trained dog will make a wonderful companion.

curiosity or appear slightly startled but should not panic, try to run away, show aggressiveness, or bark.

Test 10: Supervised Separation

This test demonstrates that your dog can be left with a trusted person if necessary and will show good manners. Evaluators are encouraged to ask something like, "Would you like me to watch your dog?" and then take hold of the dog's leash. You will then leave your dog's sight for three minutes. Your dog does not have to stay in position but should not continually bark, whine, pace unnecessarily, or show anything stronger than mild irritation or nervousness.

Part 3

Part Four
Having Fun

"Sidney! Close the door! You're letting cats in!"

14

Traveling With Your Dog

One of the best things about getting a new puppy is that you have a companion who can accompany you on any adventure. There are so many activities that you and your puppy can become involved in, from organized dog sports, to therapy and assistance work, to just plain having fun. Determine what kinds of activities your puppy is suited to and match those abilities to your interests. This way, both you and your canine friend are guaranteed to have lots of fun together.

Road Trips

The first step to getting out there and trying

Traveling with your dog is a great way Yo bond with him.

One of the safest ways for your dog to travel is in a crate.

new experiences is making sure that your pup can travel with you. Your puppy must become used to everyday travel in order to go to the veterinarian, the groomer, and even better, the dog park. Also, at some point you will have to decide whether or not the puppy will accompany the family on vacation. Puppyhood is the time to start acclimating your dog to new surroundings. The earlier you start, the better.

A puppy who has good experiences in the car from the start should have no problems. In fact, most dogs love to take a ride and will eagerly jump into the back seat. All I have to say to my dog, Chester, is, "Wanna go…?" and he's sitting by the car door. In fact, with most dogs, you can't even open the car door when they're around, because they'll jump right in and refuse to get out!

Travel Tips

The following procedures should help your puppy get used to road travel:

✔ Make sure you allow ample time outside before you and your pup get in the car. This will help prevent accidents.

✗ Do not feed your pup for a few hours before you start traveling. Also, allow for plenty of air circulation throughout the car to avoid overheating or stuffiness.

✔ Place your puppy in the car for a few moments while it is parked in the driveway. Let him out, and then offer a treat. Do this every day for about a week or until your puppy looks forward to sitting in the car. (Of course, getting the treat has a lot to do with it!)

✔ Once your puppy is content sitting in the car, drive to the end of the driveway or down the block and back. When you let him out, offer a treat. Do this for about a week or until your puppy willingly gets in the car for short rides.

✔ Once your puppy seems totally comfortable with very short rides, gradually make them longer. Always end by giving a treat or by driving a short distance to a fun destination.

It may be slow going at first, but if you are patient and make the trips fun and rewarding, your puppy will be traveling like a pro in no time.

Part 4

No Parking

Never, *ever* leave your dog unattended in a car. Temperatures can climb to life-threatening levels very quickly, even if the windows are partially rolled down and the dog has access to drinking water. Your dog can suffer from heat-stroke in a very short time, so if you can't bring your dog with you when you leave the car, leave him at home.

Your puppy should be leash trained before you travel together.

The best way to ensure that your dog has the same reaction is to make all car rides pleasant. This doesn't mean that you should never take your puppy to the vet for shots, but make sure that's not the *only* place you both go in the car, either. When you do go to the vet, the groomer, or anywhere else that may be unpleasant, make sure you also stop at the beach or park on the way home as a reward.

The safest place for your puppy when he's in the car is in a crate. They also make harnesses, dog seat belts, and barriers for the back of cars to keep your puppy safe and secure while traveling. A dog who roams all over the car can even interfere with your driving and injure you both. You can pay better attention to the road when you know that your dog is secure and safe in one spot.

Unfortunately, some dogs aren't very good travelers. Perhaps they associate the car with leaving their mother or with trips to the veterinarian. Others may be nervous riders and get carsick. These dogs need special conditioning in order to make them good travelers. The best thing to do for these pups is to slowly recondition them to enjoy the time they spend in the car.

Part 4

Preparing for Flight

Listed below are some helpful travel tips from the Animal and Plant Health Inspection Service (APHIS), an agency of the US Department of Agriculture. APHIS enforces regulations ensuring that animals traveling by air are treated humanely by airlines.

✔ If you are sending your pet through the cargo system, you will need to go to the cargo terminal, which is usually located in a separate part of the airport. Be sure to check with your airline for the acceptance cutoff time for your flight. By regulation, an animal may be present for transport no more than four hours before flight time.

✔ Use direct flights whenever possible to avoid accidental transfers or delays.

✔ Remember that some dogs are more likely to experience breathing problems during air travel, such as short-nosed breeds like Bulldogs.

✔ Instructions for feeding and watering an animal over a 24-hour period must be attached to the kennel. The 24-hour schedule will assist the airline in providing care in case your dog is diverted from the original destination.

✔ Carry a leash with you so that you can walk your pet before check-in and after arrival. Do not place the leash inside the kennel or attach it to the outside of the kennel—keep it with you.

✔ Outfit your pet with a sturdy collar and two identification tags. The tags should have both your permanent address and telephone number and an address and telephone number where you can be reached while traveling.

✔ Attach a label on the pet carrier with your permanent and travel addresses and telephone numbers.

✔ Make sure your pet's nails have been recently clipped to prevent snagging on the carrier door or other openings.

✔ Carry a current photograph of your pet. If he is accidentally lost, this will make the search easier.

✔ Most of all, don't be afraid to speak up. Let the crew know that your pet is traveling with you and that his safety is crucial.

✔ If you need to file a complaint regarding the care of your pet during transport, contact USDA-APHIS-Animal Care.

On Your Way

Once your puppy is used to traveling, life is an open road! There are many destinations in the US and in Canada that welcome canine travelers. If you decide to take an extended road trip with your puppy, the following tips will make your vacation a little easier on everyone.

Some dogs will need special conditioning to be good travelers.

Before you hit the road, your puppy should know basic obedience commands and be leash trained. Any dog should be leashed whenever out of the car. This is because you'll most likely be stopping in rest areas that have lots of traffic, and you will encounter new people and places that could possibly scare the dog. Remember to bring enough food to last the entire trip. If you run out, you might not be able to find the brand your puppy normally eats, and a quick switch in food can cause an upset stomach or diarrhea, making the trip miserable for all of you.

Pack the car not only for the humans on the trip, but also for your dog. Bring equipment like leashes, water and food dishes, favorite toys, grooming supplies, medication (if needed), a scooper and plastic bags. Don't forget to pack a first-aid kit in case your pup gets injured.

If your puppy becomes lost, make sure the information on your pet's identification tag is current, and be sure to include the phone number and address of where you'll be staying while on vacation. Tattooing identification is a good idea as well. Also remember to bring a copy of your dog's rabies certificate and inoculation record. Without it, animal control officers could impound or quarantine your dog if you run into a problem.

Pet Sitter Tips

To make sure everything runs smoothly while you're away, advanced planning is recommended. The following tips should help your pet sitter better care for your puppy:

✓ Make an extra copy of your house key for the sitter, and make sure it works. As a backup, give another copy to a neighbor. Let your sitter know the name and phone number of this neighbor.

✓ Buy extra food and supplies just in case you stay away longer than anticipated.

✓ Leave a list of phone numbers, such as your veterinarian and the place where you are staying while away.

✓ All food, leashes, and medicines should be left in one area so they are easy to locate.

✓ If the sitter will be visiting in the evenings, provide a timer light so he or she won't have to walk into a dark house. It will probably make your pet more comfortable as well.

✓ If you will be returning earlier or later than expected, call to inform your sitter.

✓ Unplug any appliances that won't be used to prevent damage during electrical storms or injury to pets.

Air Travel

Let's face it, dogs are happiest with all four feet on the ground. Airline travel can be stressful for your puppy. On some airlines, puppies and small dogs are allowed to travel with you in the cabin if they can fit under the seat and are properly contained. However, most dogs will have to fly in the cargo hold, where they can be subjected to temperature changes, flight delays, and other difficulties. Most experts recommend that your puppy does not fly, but if it cannot be avoided, there are ways to make the flight easier.

First, you need to get an airline-approved crate. Federal guidelines on crate size and construction must be adhered to. Crates need to be sturdy, properly ventilated, contain water and food dishes, and most importantly, be large enough for the animal to freely stand, turn around, and lie down. To prevent injury, no part of the animal's body should protrude through any openings of the crate. For this reason, crates made exclusively of wire are not advisable. A "Live Animal" label with letters at least one inch high must be placed on the crate, along with arrows indicating which end is up. If your dog is not crate trained, slowly introduce the crate long before the flight.

Part 4

Second, take your dog to the vet at least 30 days before you travel. Health certificates are required for all pets transported by air and are usually valid for 30 days for domestic flights and 10 days for international flights.

It is also important to advise the airline that you are traveling with an animal when you make your reservations. Be sure to reconfirm with the airline 24 to 48 hours before departure that you will be bringing your pet. Advance arrangements are not a guarantee that your animal will travel on a specific flight, so be vigilant about confirming that your pet will travel with you on the same flight all the way.

Lots of pets travel safely every year by air. If you follow the proper guidelines, air travel should be less stressful for all involved.

Leaving Your Puppy Behind

You might find it best to leave your pup at home when you travel for days at a time. There are a few options you can choose to make sure your puppy is comfortable and well taken care of when you're not there.

Pet Sitters

Pet care providers can come to your house once or twice a day to feed, walk, and play with your pet while you're away. The best part about this type of service is that animals get to stay at home where they feel most comfortable and can keep their daily routine.

When hiring a pet sitter, interview several candidates before making a decision. Remember that this person will have the responsibility for both your pet and home, so

Your dogs may be more comfortable at home if you plan to travel by air.

Part 4

Hiring a pet sitter while you're away is one possible travel option.

making the right selection is important. You should find out if the pet sitter is bonded, has commercial liability insurance, and will provide references. Ask for documented proof of these, and check references. Services offered and fees charged can vary widely depending on what state you live in or even what town.

Once you've hired a sitter, let him or her know your puppy's daily eating, sleeping, and exercising schedule. Health problems should also be disclosed, as well as any medication your pet needs.

Boarding Kennels

Placing your pet in a boarding kennel is another option if you must travel for an extended period of time. Family, friends, co-workers, and your veterinarian are all good places to start your search for a well-run boarding kennel. Find out what they liked and disliked about the establishment, as well as how long they've used the facility. Consider using the resources available to find licensed boarding kennels throughout the US.

Once you have some leads, make an unannounced visit to check out the facility. The first place you'll want to see is where the animals are kept. If you're not allowed to view this area, for whatever reason, find another place. A reputable operator should never have a problem with showing the facility to a potential client; it could indicate a disorganized, unkempt place.

Most importantly, ask if the facility accepts puppies. Also ask if it accepts puppies who are on medication or who require special handling, if necessary. If they do, find out if there is an extra fee for these special cases.

As you tour the kennel, you'll want to take note of a few things. The fencing used for runs should be in good shape and smooth, with no sharp edges. There should be a solid barrier between runs high enough to prevent physical contact and cross urination. Also, if you have an escape artist puppy, make sure the runs have covers and that the bottoms of the fences are secure. The sleeping area of a run should be roomy enough for your pet to stand up comfortably, turn around in, and easily stretch out.

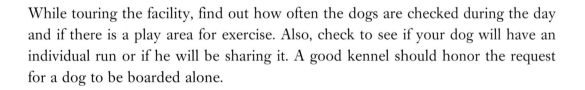
Check to make sure that the facility you choose accepts puppies.

Overall, the facility should be clean, well lit, and odorless. Kennels should be disinfected daily with a cleaning solution, like diluted bleach, then rinsed thoroughly and allowed to dry before an animal is let back into the run to prevent chemical burns. The temperature should be set to a comfortable level. There should also be a good ventilation system, which allows fresh air to circulate into the kennel area.

While touring the facility, find out how often the dogs are checked during the day and if there is a play area for exercise. Also, check to see if your dog will have an individual run or if he will be sharing it. A good kennel should honor the request for a dog to be boarded alone.

Ask what brand of food is used. Some facilities only stock one type, while others have several popular varieties in order to match their clients' regular fare. If they don't have your dog's brand, find out if you can bring in a supply. Sticking with your dog's regular diet is important, because a sudden change can cause an upset stomach and/or diarrhea.

Find out how they handle health situations and veterinary procedures. What is their policy if the kennel staff notices any health problems, such as vomiting, dehydration,

A good kennel should be clean and well lit.

Find out in advance what kind of food the kennel provides.

or bloody stool or urine? Will they take the dog to your regular veterinarian or use their own?

Check which methods of payment they accept and what their hours of operation are. Some facilities might be closed on weekends and certain holidays, which means if you return home on those days, you won't be able to pick up your pet until the next day.

Usually boarders are required to be vaccinated for rabies, distemper, parvovirus, hepatitis, leptospirosis, parainfluenza, and bordetella or kennel cough. Ask if there are any other types of vaccinations required and what proof you'll need to show that your dog has had the proper immunizations.

After your visit and before making a decision on what facility to use, take into consideration whether the staff was friendly and if the establishment was well run and organized. The more you know about the facility, the easier you will feel about your puppy's welfare while you are away.

The Ambitious Puppy

Once your puppy has completed basic obedience training, there are many different activities that you can participate in together. Almost all dogs have special skills for which they were originally bred. The trick is to find the perfect match: Find the sport that your dog has a natural talent for and enjoys doing and that you enjoy doing together. Once you find that perfect combination, there is no end to how far you and your puppy can go.

Activities and Service

Not all dog sports have to be organized events. Your puppy will be happy to join you and your

There are many activities in which you and your dog can participate together.

Many dogs enjoy outdoor activities.

Lyme Lights

If you go hiking or camping with your puppy, be aware that there are certain areas of the country that have a high incidence of Lyme disease. If you plan to travel to any of the following regions, talk to your veterinarian to see if a vaccination is needed for protection: Connecticut, Massachusetts, Rhode Island, Westchester and Duchess Counties in New York, northern California, Wisconsin, Michigan's upper peninsula, and northern Illinois are all areas with a high incidence of Lyme.

family in almost any activity. However, it is important to remember that very young puppies are still growing; their bones are soft, and they may not be fully developed until they are a year old or more. Hold off on any serious workouts until your puppy has fully matured physically, as he may suffer permanent damage.

Dogs thrive on exercise and will be happy to accompany you jogging, walking, or bicycling. Some breeds, like Newfoundlands and retrievers, make exceptional swimmers and can be trained for water rescue. Others will enjoy camping, backpacking, and hiking–whatever recreation you are interested in, there is a dog who can do it.

As with any form of exercise, make sure your dog is warmed up first and builds stamina slowly. Of course, you can't expect a Chihuahua to accompany you on a 10-mile run, so also take into consideration any physical limitations. Hopefully, you have chosen your puppy with this in mind. If you take the proper precautions, your dog can be in the best physical shape–like any conditioned athlete–and you will have a great workout companion.

Part 4

Carting and Draft Dogs

In many parts of the world, beasts of burden like horses and oxen were not easy to come by. Therefore, breeds like the Newfoundland, Bouvier des Flandres, Alaskan Malamute, and Bernese Mountain Dog have been used for thousands of years as cart pullers, sled dogs, and draft dogs. These breeds can still show their inherent talents and strength by participating in sled and carting competitions and draft tests. If your breed is one that historically has had this ability and is physically fit, you can contact the breed club in your area to find out more about how to begin training for these events. Once trained, your dog can use these skills not only in organized events, but also in helping you with hauling and yard work.

Therapy Dogs

There is nothing more rewarding than seeing someone else get as much happiness and delight out of your puppy as you do, and there are some dogs who just seem to love getting a smile out of anyone and everyone. Getting involved with therapy work is a wonderful way to spread the joy of dog ownership to those who may benefit most from it. Statistics show that therapy dogs are creating some remarkable results with the sick, the elderly, and people with special needs. If your puppy has a particularly even and friendly temperament, therapy work may be perfect for him and especially rewarding for you.

You and your dog can visit the elderly in nursing homes or patients in hospitals or enroll in a program to educate children about the care and training of dogs. If you contact a therapy program or your local humane society, they can better inform you of

Dogs with pleasant, friendly temperaments may be perfect for therapy work.

Part 4

Assistance dogs are trained to help people with physical disabilities.

Search and rescue dogs find victims and survivors at disaster scenes.

programs in your area and the best way to get started. A therapy dog can make a valuable contribution to the quality of life of others.

Assistance Dogs

Some puppies can be trained to assist people with physical disabilities. They can help the blind get around independently, help the deaf hear the telephone or the doorbell, and help those confined to wheelchairs accomplish everyday activities like opening doors or getting items they need. There are special programs that screen and train these puppies, as well as foster programs for people who can take in puppies to train and socialize them until they are ready to be placed with that special person.

Search and Rescue Dogs

In almost any city, you will find a canine search and rescue unit. These dedicated handlers and their dogs go to scenes of disasters to help find survivors and victims. They also help find people who may be lost. These handler/dog teams travel great distances and give up much of their time and energy to help others. They do this for the personal sense of satisfaction that they receive, not for money or glory.

It takes a special dog and owner to devote so much of themselves to helping others. Search and rescue dogs come in all different breeds, but all have a few traits in common: athleticism, tracking ability, and perseverance.

Part 4

Getting your dog certified as a search and rescue dog is not easy. You must go through rigorous training exercises under the same conditions that the dog will be facing before you are allowed to actually go to work. The best way to get started is to contact your local law enforcement agency or one of the national associations to see if there are any units in your area. The next time disaster strikes, you and your dog could be helping others—and there is no greater reward of dog ownership.

Part 4

Organized Dog Sports and Events

Conformation

Everyone thinks that they have a good-looking puppy. If your dog is an AKC-registered purebred and is six months of age or older, you may want to jump into the world of dog showing. You may have even purchased your puppy from a breeder with the intent of getting into conformation. In conformation, the main consideration is overall appearance and structure and how closely the dog conforms to the official standard of perfection for the breed.

If you would like to get involved in showing,

Most dogs can participate in a variety of sports.

Conformation showing is based on the standard for the breed.

the first thing you should do is go to dog shows in your area without your dog. Spend the day watching not only your breed's judging but others as well. Judges examine the dogs and place them according to how close each one compares with the ideal dog as described in the breed's official standard. These judges are experts in the breeds they are judging. They examine each dog with their hands to see if the teeth, muscles, bones, and coat texture match the standard. Each dog is examined in profile for general balance and watched while moving to see how all these features fit together.

There are three types of conformation shows: Specialty, Group, and All-breed. Specialty shows are limited to a specific breed. Group shows are limited

Classes in Conformation

Class	Age Group	Qualifications
Puppy	6- & under 12- month-old dogs	Not yet champions
12 – 18 Months	12-to 18-month-old dogs	Not yet champions
Novice	ages over 6 months	Never won a blue ribbon in any other class or fewer than three blue ribbons in the novice class under one year that are not yet champions
Bred by Exhibitor	ages over 6 months	Dogs who have been bred by the same person exhibiting them
American Bred	ages over 6 months	Dogs from a breeding that took place in America and who were born in America
Open	ages over 6 months	Open to any dog of that breed

to dogs from one of the seven groups (for example, an all-terrier show). All-breed shows are open to the 150 breeds (at the time of this printing) recognized by the AKC. Most dogs at conformation shows are competing for points toward a championship. It takes 15 points, including two major wins (3, 4, or 5 points) under at least three different judges to become an AKC Champion of Record, which is indicated by a "Ch." before the dog's name.

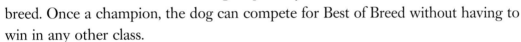

Only the Best of Breed conformation winners will advance to the Group competition.

At one show, a non-champion dog can earn from one to five points, depending on the number actually defeated. There are six different regular classes in which dogs may be entered, and these are offered to male and female dogs separately in each breed. Once a champion, the dog can compete for Best of Breed without having to win in any other class.

After these classes are judged, the first-place winner in each class competes for the championship points. This is done separately for male and female dogs. Only the best male, Winners Dog, and the best female, Winners Bitch, receive championship points. A Reserve Winner award is given in each sex to the runner-up. The Winners Dog and the Winners Bitch then compete with the champions for Best of Breed. At the end of the Best of Breed competition, three awards are usually given. Best of Breed is given to the dog judged best in each breed. Best of Winners is awarded to either the Winners Dog or the Winners Bitch, and Best of Opposite Sex is given to the best of the opposite sex to the Best of Breed winner.

Only the Best of Breed winners advance to compete in the Group competition. Each breed falls into one of seven Group classifications. Four placements are awarded in each Group, but only the first place winner advances to the Best in Show competition.

Dog showing can be a very rewarding experience. But be careful—once bitten by the show bug, many people get addicted!

Junior Showmanship

If your children are interested in training and competing, you may want to get involved in Junior Showmanship, which evolved as part of the concept that dog shows should be a family sport as well as entertainment. It was started in the 1930s and has continually grown in participation. It is now an integral part of almost every dog show held in the US and other countries. It is a great way to teach children how to handle, care for, and respect their pets, and also gives them a good start in the sport of dog showing. Participating in Junior Showmanship deepens the unique relationship between children and their dogs.

Dog showing is a rewarding experience for you and your dog.

The American Kennel Club rules state that the dog entered in a Junior Showmanship class must be owned by the junior, a member of the immediate family, or someone from the same household. Every dog entered must be eligible to compete in either conformation or obedience, which means the dog must be registered with the AKC. This does not mean that the dog must be of top quality. The rules state that entries in this activity are not judged on the quality of the dog but on the ability of the junior handler only.

The classes are Novice Junior and Novice Senior, and Open Junior and Open Senior. The Novice Junior class is for boys and girls who are at least 10 but under 14 years of age on the day of the show and who have not won three first-place awards in a Novice class at a licensed or member show. The Novice Senior class is for boys and girls who are at least 14 but under 18 years of age and who have not won three first-place awards in a Novice class. The Open Junior class is for boys and girls who are at least 10 but under 14 years of age on the day of the show and who have won three first-place awards in a Novice class. The Open Senior class is for boys and girls who are at least 14 but under 18 years of age on the day of the show and have won three first-place awards in a Novice class.

Obedience

You may find that your puppy aced puppy kindergarten and loves to work with you practicing basic commands. If you have a "workaholic" pup on your hands, obedience may be the right event for you.

Obedience trials test your dog's ability to perform a particular set of exercises. The handler and dog team is scored on performance. In each exercise, you must score more than 50 percent of the possible points (ranging from 20 to 40) and get a total score of at least 170 out of a possible 200. Each time you do this, your dog gets a "leg" toward a title. Three legs under three different judges and your dog earns an obedience title.

There are three title levels, and each is more difficult than the one before. You may see levels divided into "A" and "B"; "A" classes are for beginners whose dogs have never received a title, while "B" classes are for more experienced handlers. The three levels are Novice, Open, and Utility. The dogs who earn their Utility degrees can go on to compete for a UDX (Utility Dog Excellent) or OTCh. (Obedience Trial Championship).

The first level, Novice, requires the skills for a good canine companion. Dogs will have to heel both on and off leash at different speeds, come when called,

Obedience trials test your dog's ability to perform a certain set of exercises.

Dog sports are a great way to keep your dog in shape.

Tracking tests involve following a particular scent.

stay with a group of other dogs, and stand for a simple physical exam. Dogs who qualify will earn a CD (Companion Dog) title after their names.

The second level, Open, requires many of the same exercises as in the Novice class, but off leash and for longer periods of time. There are also jumping and retrieving tasks. Dogs who qualify will earn a CDX (Companion Dog Excellent) title.

The final level, Utility, consists of more difficult exercises, including scent discrimination tasks. Dogs who qualify will earn a UD (Utility Dog) title.

Tracking

All dogs love to use their noses to communicate with people and other dogs every day. Tracking tests allow dogs to demonstrate their natural ability to recognize and follow scent. This vigorous outdoor activity is especially great for canine athletes who have an affinity for tracking, such as some dogs in the Hound Group. Unlike obedience, your dog only has to pass one tracking test in order to earn this title.

There are three titles that a dog can earn in tracking events. The first is the TD or Tracking Dog title. Dogs can earn a TD by following a track laid down by a human 30 minutes to 2 hours before. The rules describe certain turns in a 440- to 500-yard track. The second title, TDX, or Tracking Dog Excellent, is earned by following an older (laid down three to five hours before) and longer (800 to

Part 4

Tracking

A good way to get your dog started in tracking is to play hide-and-seek in the house. Begin with the name of a certain toy that your dog likes, such as a ball. First, hide the ball, but let the dog see where you put it. Then say, "Find it." After the dog gets the hang of it, put him in another room while you hide the object. You can make the game increasingly difficult by using different objects. If your pet enjoys playing hide-and-seek, you probably have a natural tracking dog on your hands.

Dogs can earn three tracking events titles.

1,000 yards) track with more turns while overcoming both physical and scenting obstacles. A dog who has earned a VST or Variable Surface Tracking title has demonstrated the ability to track through urban and wilderness settings by successfully following a three- to-five-hour-old track that may go down a street, through buildings, or through other areas devoid of vegetation.

Agility

One of the fastest growing, most popular, and fun events is agility. It was developed and introduced in 1978 in England by John Varley and Peter Meanwell as an entertaining diversion between judgings at dog shows, but it was officially recognized as a sport by the AKC in the early 1980s. Agility is an exciting sport in

Agility was first developed as a diversion between judgings at dog shows.

which you guide your dog off-lead using verbal commands and hand signals over a series of obstacles on a timed course.

Agility trial titles are Novice Agility Dog (NAD), Open Agility Dog (OAD), Agility Dog Excellent (ADX), and Master Agility Excellent (MAX). In order to acquire an agility title, your dog must earn three qualifying scores in each class under two different judges. The MAX title is awarded after the dog earns ten qualifying scores in the Agility Excellent Class.

Agility clubs can provide you with information about the sport.

The only problem with training your puppy to compete in agility is finding the equipment and space to train. Many agility clubs can provide information on getting started toward an agility title. Even if you don't compete, just training for agility can be lots of fun for both you and your dog.

Flyball

Is your puppy an athletic, active dog with a special affinity for tennis balls? If so, flyball may be the right sport for you and your buddy. Flyball is a relay race between two teams, each with four dogs and four handlers. Each dog takes a turn running over a course with four jumps and a flyball box at the end of the course. The dog presses a pedal on the front of a flyball box. This releases a throwing arm that sends a tennis ball up in the air. The dog catches the ball and runs back over the course to the starting line. Then the next dog runs. The first team to have all four dogs successfully complete the course is the winner. It is an exciting sport, and you may find that it allows your puppy to turn his abilities into a pastime that's fun for all involved.

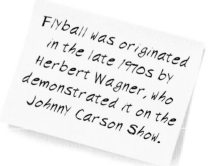

Flyball was originated in the late 1970s by Herbert Wagner, who demonstrated it on the Johnny Carson Show.

Frisbee™

Some dogs just love to play Frisbee™; they sleep with it, eat with it, and live to play the next game of fetch. People have taken this and developed a sport that allows dogs to display their amazing athletic aptitude. It all started in the mid-1970s when Alex Stein ran out on the field in the middle of a Dodgers baseball game and performed with his Frisbee™ dog, Ashley Whippet. A nationwide audience got to enjoy the high-flying demonstration on television, and the sport of canine Frisbee™ was born.

Good Frisbee™ dogs have strong retrieving and tracking instincts.

Both mixed-breed and purebred dogs can compete, but dogs who excel at Frisbee™ are medium-sized, lean, agile dogs who are able to take flying leaps and use their owners as launching pads. Other characteristics that make a good Frisbee™ dog are strong retrieving and tracking instincts, an even temperament, and sound hips.

Frisbee™ competitions are held all over the country. They are divided into beginner and intermediate levels, each consisting of two different events. The first event is called the mini-distance, which is played on a 20-yard field. Competitors are given 60 seconds to make as many throws and catches as possible. The second event is the free-flight event that consists of a

Training for dog sports can be a lot of fun.

choreographed series of acrobatic moves to music. Judges award points on a one to ten scale in each of the following categories: degree of difficulty, execution, leaping agility, and showmanship. Bonus points can be given to competitors with spectacular or innovative free-flight moves.

Friskies® and Alpo® sponsor over 100 community contests throughout the country each year. There are also seven regional qualifying tournaments culminating in the invitational World Finals at the mall in Washington, DC.

Earthdog Trials

Does your terrier or Dachshund pup love to dig holes and chase rabbits in your backyard? If so, you may have a natural candidate for earthdog trials. Earthdog trials are for the "go-to-ground" breeds (the smaller terriers and Dachshunds) that were originally bred to go into dens and tunnels after prey, which consisted of all types of small vermin, from rats to badgers. There are four class levels at a licensed trial: Introduction to Quarry (for beginning handlers and dogs), Junior Earthdog, Senior Earthdog, and Master Earthdog. The object of the test is to give your dog an opportunity to display the ability to follow game and to "work" the quarry. The "work" is showing interest in the game by barking, digging, and scratching. The quarry can either be two adult rats, who must be caged to be protected from the dogs, or artificial quarry that is located behind a barrier, properly scented, and capable of movement. The dogs eligible to participate in earthdog trials are Dachshunds, as well as Australian, Bedlington, Border, Cairn, Dandie Dinmont, Fox (Smooth and Wire), Lakeland, Norfolk, Norwich, Parson Russell, Scottish, Sealyham, Silky, Skye, Welsh, and West Highland White.

Individual clubs sponsor field events under AKC sanction or license.

Part 4

Field Events

The American Kennel Club runs field trials and hunt tests that are open to pointing breeds, retrievers, spaniels, Basset Hounds, Beagles, and Dachshunds over the age of six months and registered with the AKC. Individual clubs sponsor these events under AKC sanction or license. If you own any of the eligible breeds, it is quite a thrill to see your puppy develop and demonstrate those natural instincts.

Hunt tests judge the dog's ability to perform against a standard of perfection.

In hunt tests, the dog's ability to perform is judged against a standard of perfection established by AKC regulations. Dogs who receive qualifying scores at a number of tests achieve titles of JH (Junior Hunter), SH (Senior Hunter), and MH (Master Hunter), each successively requiring more skill.

In field trials, dogs compete against each other for placements and points toward field championships. Successful dogs earn an FC (Field Champion) title in front of their names. The field events are divided by subgroups of dogs and are sometimes limited to specific breeds. Each type of event varies according to a breed's function. These events include:

Beagling: Currently, there are three types of trials: Brace, the oldest, is run in braces of two or three dogs who are judged primarily on their accuracy

Field events vary according to a breed's function.

Part 4

Pointing breeds must demonstrate their ability to find, point, and retrieve downed birds.

Field events are sometimes limited to specific breeds.

trailing a rabbit; Small Pack Option (SPO), which divides the dogs into packs of seven to pursue rabbits; and Large Pack, which turn all the dogs in the class loose to find and track hares.

Basset Hounds and Dachshunds: These trials are run in a similar fashion as the Beagle Brace trials but are held separately.

Pointing Breeds: The AKC offers pointing breed field trials and hunt tests. The dogs are run in braces around a course on which birds are released. Dogs must demonstrate their ability to find birds, point, and retrieve the downed birds. The eligible pointing breeds are the Brittany, English Setter, German Shorthaired Pointer, Pointer, Gordon Setter, Irish Setter, Vizsla, Weimaraner, and Wirehaired Pointing Griffon.

Retrievers: Retrievers are tested on their ability to remember or "mark" the location of downed birds and to return the birds to their handlers. Both the hunt tests and the field trials have different levels of difficulty, requiring dogs to mark multiple birds and find unmarked birds, called blind retrieves. Breeds that are eligible for these trials are the Chesapeake, Curly-Coated, Flat Coated, Golden, and Labrador Retrievers, and the Irish Water Spaniel.

Spaniels: Spaniels are judged on their natural and learned ability to hunt, flush, and retrieve game on both land and water. Breeds that are eligible for hunt tests are the Clumber, Cocker, English Cocker, English Springer, Sussex, and Welsh Springer Spaniels. Presently, only Cocker, English Cocker, and English Springer Spaniels are eligible to compete in field trials.

The AKC has licensed Beagle Field Trials for more than 105 years.

Herding Trials

If your breed is in the Herding Group (or is a Samoyed or Rottweiler), you may have noticed your dog circling or "rounding up" bicycles, birds, or even your children. This inherent ability to control livestock can be put to good use by participating in herding tests and/or trials. Herding trials are designed to allow your dog to demonstrate the ability to herd under the direction of a handler. Your puppy must be at least nine months old and one of the following breeds to be eligible: Australian Cattle Dog, Australian Shepherd, Bearded Collie, Belgian Malinois, Belgian Sheepdog, Belgian Turvuren, Border Collie, Bouvier des Flandres, Briard, Canaan Dog, Collie, German Shepherd Dog, Old English Sheepdog, Puli, Shetland Sheepdog, Cardigan Welsh Corgi, Pembroke Welsh Corgi, Samoyed, or Rottweiler.

Herding trials test a dog's ability to control livestock.

In herding trials, your dog will be judged against a set of standards and can earn advanced titles and championships by competing against other dogs for placements. Livestock used at the trials include sheep, cattle, ducks, or goats. The titles offered are HS (Herding Started), HI (Herding Intermediate), and HX (Herding Excellent). Upon the completion of an HX, a herding championship may be earned after accumulating 15 championship points. There are also noncompetitive herding clinics and instinct tests given by AKC clubs across the country.

Part 4

Lure Coursing

There is nothing more exciting than seeing your dog do what he was bred to do, especially if that dog is a sighthound racing at full speed. Lure coursing is an event in which dogs follow an artificial lure around a course on an open field. They are scored on speed, enthusiasm, agility, endurance, and their ability to follow the lure. Eligible breeds are the Whippet, Basenji, Greyhound, Afghan Hound, Borzoi, Ibizan Hound, Pharaoh Hound, Irish Wolfhound, Scottish Deerhound, Saluki, and Rhodesian Ridgeback.

No matter what you and your puppy eventually decide to do, you will have the joy of knowing that you are doing it together. As long as your puppy is well loved, there is nothing you both can't accomplish.

There are boundless activities in which you and your dog can participate.

Part 4

Organizations

American Herding Breed Association (AHBA)
Membership Coordinator: Siouxsan Isen
E-mail: siouxsan@ahba-herding.org
www.ahba-herding.org

American Kennel Club (AKC)
5580 Centerview Drive
Raleigh, NC 27606
Telephone: (919) 233-9767
Fax: (919) 233-3627
E-mail: info@akc.org
www.akc.org

American Sighthound Field Association (ASFA)
Corresponding Secretary: Russ Jacobs
E-mail: corressecy@asfa.org
www.asfa.org

Association of Pet Dog Trainers (APDT)
5096 Sand Road SE
Iowa City, IA 52240-8217
Telephone: (800) PET-DOGS
Fax: (856) 439-0525
E-mail: information@apdt.com
www.apdt.com

British Sighthound Field Association (BSFA)
Secretary: Gary Peskett
E-mail: info@lurecoursing.org.uk
www.lurecoursing.org.uk

Canadian Kennel Club (CKC)
89 Skyway Avenue, Suite 100
Etobicoke, Ontario
M9W 6R4
Telephone: (416) 675-5511
Fax: (416) 675-6506
E-mail: information@ckc.ca
www.ckc.ca

Delta Society
580 Naches Avenue, SW Suite 101
Renton, WA 98055-2297
Telephone: (425) 226-7357
Fax: (425) 235-1076
E-mail: info@deltasociety.org
www.deltasociety.org

International Agility Link (IAL)
Global Administrator: Steve Drinkwater
E-mail: yunde@powerup.au
www.dogpatch.org/agility/IAL/ial.html

National Association of Dog Obedience Instructors, Inc. (NADOI)
PMB 369
729 Grapevine Hwy.
Hurst, TX 76054-2085
E-mail: corrsec@nadoi.org
www.nadoi.org

Veterinary Resources

American Animal Hospital Association (AAHA)
P.O. Box 150899
Denver, CO 80215-0899
Telephone: (303) 986-2800
Fax: (303) 986-1700
E-mail: info@aahanet.org
www.aahanet.org/Index.cfm

American Veterinary Medical Association (AVMA)
1931 North Meacham Road-Suite 100
Schaumburg, IL 60173
Telephone: (847) 925-8070
Fax: (847) 925-1329
E-mail: avmainfo@avma.org
www.avma.org

British Veterinary Association (BVA)
7 Mansfield Street
London
W1G 9NQ
Telephone: 020 76366541
Fax: 020 74362970
E-mail: bvahq@bva.co.uk
www.bva.co.uk

Index

A

Accidents, 120
Activities, 34, 41 162, 203-207
    agility, 19, 30, 31, 41, 65, 215-216, 222
    Canine Good Citizen® test, 187-190
    dog shows, 210, 212
    earthdog, 19, 218
    field trials, 65
    flyball, 19, 31, 216
    Frisbee™, 217-218
    herding, 19, 30
    hunting, 34
    lure coursing, 19, 222
    obedience, 13, 19, 30, 31, 41, 46, 47, 65, 182,
        212, 213-214
    search and rescue, 24, 26, 31, 88, 206-207
    sled dogs, 26
    therapy and assistance, 24, 26, 31, 41, 88, 205-206
    tracking, 214-215
Activity level, 19, 22, 23, 29
Adoption, 21, 31, 37, 38, 105
Affection, 73, 74
Affenpinscher, 28
Afghan Hound, 25, 222

Aggression, 31, 34, 46, 76, 78, 82, 83, 85, 86, 87,
    106, 110, 180, 184, 190, 183
Agility, 19, 30, 31, 41, 65, 215-216, 222
Airedale Terrier, 27
Air travel, 53, 198-199
Akita, 22, 26, 31
Alaskan Malamute, 26, 205
Allergic reactions, 109
Alpha, 72, 73, 82, 85
America, 210
American Eskimo Dog, 29
American Foxhound, 25
American Heartworm Society, 103
American Kennel Club (AKC), 23, 24, 25, 26, 27,
    28, 30, 31, 38, 187, 209, 211, 212, 215, 219, 220,
    221
American Staffordshire Terrier, 27
American Water Spaniel, 23
Anatolian Shepherd Dog, 26
Anemia, 100, 104, 111
Anesthesia, 112, 122
Animal and Plant Health Inspection Service
    (APHIS), 196

Annual checkup, 98

Assistance dog(s), 24, 41, 206

Association of American Feed Control Officials
    (AAFCO), 129, 130

Association of Pet Dog Trainers (APDT), 165

Australian Cattle Dog, 30, 221

Australian Shepherd, 19, 22, 30, 31, 51, 94, 221

Australian Terrier, 27, 218

B

Baby gate, 51, 54

Barking, 36, 73, 78, 79, 80, 81, 85, 157, 177-179,
    185, 190

Basenji, 25, 140, 222

Basic commands, 167, 213
    come, 125, 167, 168-169, 176, 182, 189
    down, 167, 171, 172-174, 184, 189
    heel, 167, 174-175, 213
    no, 176
    sit, 78, 79, 85, 86, 125, 167, 169-171, 173, 179,
        184, 188, 189
    stay, 167, 171-172, 189, 214

Basic training, 79, 86, 161-190

Basset Hound, 24, 25, 31, 219, 220

Bathing, 143, 144

Beagle, 25, 31, 51, 125, 219

Bearded Collie, 30, 221

Bedlington Terrier, 27, 126, 218

Bee stings, 121

Behavior, 78, 80, 110, 112, 125

Belgian Malinois, 30, 221

Belgian Sheepdog, 30, 221

Belgian Turvuren, 30, 221

Bernese Mountain Dog, 26, 205

Bichon Frise, 29, 127, 140

Bites, 13, 31, 109, 120

Biting, 37, 46, 47, 180-181

Black and Tan Coonhound, 25

Black Russian Terrier, 26

Bleeding, 116-117, 120, 145

Bloat, 124

Bloodhound, 25

Boarding kennels, 99, 200-202

Body language, 73, 81

Bones, 137, 180, 181

Booster vaccination, 100, 107

Border Collie, 19, 22, 30, 221

Border Terrier, 27, 218

Bordetella (kennel cough), 99, 202

Bordetella vaccine, 97, 100

Boredom, 19, 135, 137, 173, 179, 186

Borzoi, 25, 222

Boston Terrier, 29

Bouvier des Flandres, 30, 205, 221

Boxer, 26, 31

Breed clubs, 36, 187, 205

Breeder(s), 22, 23, 30, 50, 52, 63, 64, 66, 67, 76,
    80, 83, 84, 95, 96, 105, 106, 125, 134, 135, 165,
    209

Briard, 30, 221

Brittany, 23, 220

Brushing, 139, 142-143

Brussels Griffon, 28

Bull Terrier (colored, white), 27

Bulldog, 19, 29, 118, 147

Bullmastiff, 26

C

Cairn Terrier, 27, 218

Canaan Dog, 30, 221

Canada, 197

Canine Eye Registration Foundation (CERF®), 34

Canine Good Citizen® test, 187-190

Canine parvovirus, 64

Capillary refill time (CRT), 111, 117

Car ride, 50

Carbohydrates, 128, 129

Cardiac arrest, 116

Cardigan Welsh Corgi, 30, 221

Carsickness, 63, 195

Cataracts, 34

Cavalier King Charles Spaniel, 28

Characteristics, 21, 29, 46

Chesapeake Bay Retriever, 23, 34, 144, 220

Chewing, 54, 55, 59, 111, 137, 176, 180

Chew toys, 112

Cheyletiella, 102-103

Chihuahua, 28, 204

Children, 16, 36, 46, 47, 50, 60, 61, 77, 83, 84, 87, 88, 95, 131, 159, 162, 177, 183, 184, 186, 187, 212, 221

Chinese Crested, 28, 140

Chinese Shar-Pei, 29, 147

Choking, 117-118

Chow Chow, 29, 111, 140

Clumber Spaniel, 23, 221

Coat, 17, 18, 40, 141, 142, 143, 210

Coat type, 16, 18, 22, 29, 140-141

Coccidia, 105

Cocker Spaniel, 31, 94, 221

Cocker Spaniel (American), 23

Collar, 51, 52, 64, 79, 175, 176, 196

Collar training, 166-167

Collie, 30, 127, 140, 221

Come, 125, 167, 168-169, 176, 182, 189

Command(s), 51, 76, 78, 86, 152, 155

   come, 125, 167, 168-169, 176, 182, 189

   down, 167, 171, 172-174, 184, 189

   heel, 167, 174-175, 213

   no, 176

   sit, 78, 79, 85, 86, 125, 167, 169-171, 173, 179, 184, 188, 189

   stay, 167, 171-172, 189, 214

Compulsive training, 163-164

Conformation, 65, 209-212

Coprophagia, 186-187

Coronavirus, 99

Coronavirus vaccine, 100

Coughing, 40, 104, 108

CPR, 116, 118, 121

Crate(s), 51, 53-54, 68, 100, 154, 155, 156, 158, 159, 178, 180, 186, 195, 198

Crate location, 156

Crate training, 154, 198

Crying, 185

   when eliminating, 108

   when touched, 108

Curly-Coated Retriever, 23, 220

Cuts, 109

D

Dachshund, 19, 31, 125, 140, 218, 219, 220

Dachshunds, Miniature, 25

Dachshunds, Standard, 25

Dalmatian, 29, 126

Dandie Dinmont Terrier, 27, 218

Demodectic mange, 102

Dental care, 111-113, 147-148

Depression, 99

DHLPP vaccine, 96, 97, 100

Diarrhea, 40, 52, 66, 97, 98, 99, 104, 105, 107, 108, 127, 134, 197, 201

Diet, 95, 96, 123, 126, 131, 133, 135, 201

Diet sheet, 66, 133, 134, 135

Digging, 177, 181

Diseases, 36, 65, 96, 97-103, 107, 110

Distemper, 64, 96, 97-98, 202

Distemper vaccine, 97

Doberman Pinscher, 22, 26, 31, 140

Dog bite, 121, 180

Dog run, 14, 15, 59, 181

Dog shows, 210, 212

Dominance, 46, 72, 75, 76, 79, 131

Down, 167, 171, 172-174, 184, 189

Draft dogs, 26

Drinking, 156

Drowning, 118

E

Ear care, 146-147

Ear infection, 146, 147

Earthdog, 19, 218

Eating, 13, 55, 109, 119, 131, 134, 156

Electrocution, 121

Emergency, 50, 93, 115, 120

    bites, 13, 31, 109, 120

    bleeding, 116-117, 120, 145

    bloat, 124

    choking, 117-118

    CPR, 116, 118, 121

    electrocution, 121

    first-aid kit, 115, 116, 197

    heatstroke, 118-119

    poison, 119

    shock, 117

English Cocker Spaniel, 23, 221

English Foxhound, 25

English Setter, 23, 220

English Springer Spaniel, 23, 94, 221

English Toy Spaniel, 28

Examination, 109

Exercise, 11, 13, 14, 16, 18, 19, 24, 27, 30, 64, 88, 104, 124, 159, 177, 179, 201, 204

External parasites, 100-103, 104

Eye care, 147

Eye diseases, 34

Eye injuries, 109

F

Fainting, 109

Family, 11, 12, 14, 16, 17, 18, 24, 31, 38, 41, 57, 59, 60, 72, 73, 77, 78, 87, 154, 162, 179, 180, 200, 204

Fat, 128, 129, 131

Fear, 34, 39, 50, 68, 75, 76, 183-184

Feeding, 11, 159, 186

Feeding and nutrition, 123-137

Feeding schedule, 67, 134, 135, 136, 157

Fenced-in yard, 14, 181

Fences, 59

Field events, 19, 219-221

Field Spaniel, 23

Finnish Spitz, 29

First aid, 115-122

First-aid kit, 115, 116, 197

First checkup, 95-97

Flat-Coated Retriever, 23, 220

Fleabite, 100

Fleabite allergy, 100

Fleas, 100-101, 104, 105, 145

Flyball, 19, 31, 216

Food and Drug Administration Center for
Veterinary Medicine, 129

Food, 51, 52, 66, 72, 74, 95, 104, 111, 112, 119,
123, 124, 125, 127, 131, 132, 135, 136, 181, 185,
198, 201

ingredients, 130-131

labels, 129-132

net quantity statement, 132

nutritional adequacy statement, 132

types, 129

Food bowl, 51-52, 125, 155, 186, 197

Food guarding, 185-186

Foot care, 144-146

Fox Terrier (Smooth and Wire), 218

Free feeding, 135

French Bulldog, 29

Frisbee™, 217-218

G

Gazette, 41

Genetic defects, 35, 36

German Pinscher, 26

Shepherd Dog, 13, 22, 30, 31, 94, 124, 127, 221

German Shorthaired Pointer, 23, 220

German Wirehaired Pointer, 23

Giant Schnauzer, 26

Giardia, 105

Golden Retriever, 22, 23, 24, 94, 124, 220

Gordon Setter, 23, 220

Great Dane, 15, 26, 94, 124, 179

Great Pyrenees, 26, 94, 144

Greater Swiss Mountain Dog, 26

Greyhound, 25, 222

Groomer, 99, 146, 165, 188, 194, 195

Grooming, 11, 13, 18, 23, 28, 139-148, 159, 188

bathing, 143, 144

brushing, 139, 142-143

ear care, 146-147

eye care, 147

nail care, 144-146

Grooming table, 142

Grooming tools, 51, 54, 141

Guaranteed analysis, 131-132

H

Hand signals, 169, 171

Harrier, 25

Havanese, 28

Health care, 73, 93-113

Health certificate, 199

Health guarantee, 66-67

Heartworm, 103

Heartworm disease, 105

Heatstroke, 118-119

Heel, 167, 174-175, 213

Heimlich maneuver, 117

Hepatitis, 64, 96, 98, 202

Hepatitis vaccine, 97

Herding, 19, 30

Herding Group, 29-30, 127, 221

Herding Group breeds, 25, 30

Herding trials, 221

Hip dysplasia, 34, 124, 126, 127, 133, 136

Homemade diets, 132-133

Hookworms, 104

Hound Group, 24, 125, 214

Hounds, 146

Housetraining, 13, 36, 53, 106, 151-160, 186

Humane society, 37, 38, 50, 67, 106, 205

Humane Society of the United States, 37
Hypoglycemia, 126

I

Ibizan Hound, 25, 222
Identification, 53
ID tag, 50, 51, 52-53, 196, 197
Immunizations, 36, 96-97, 202
Inducive training, 164-165
Inoculation record, 64-65, 67, 197
Inoculation schedule, 36, 93
Intestinal parasites, 96, 103-105
Irish Setter, 23, 51, 124, 220
Irish Terrier, 27
Irish Water Spaniel, 23, 220
Irish Wolfhound, 25, 222
Italian Greyhound, 28

J

Japanese Chin, 28
Jumping up, 55, 79, 157, 177, 179
Junior Showmanship, 212-213

K

Keeshond, 29, 94
Kennel club, 66
Kerry Blue Terrier, 27
Komondor, 26
Kuvasz, 26

L

Labrador Retriever, 23, 24, 31, 51, 94, 140, 220
Lakeland Terrier, 27, 218
Leadership, 46

Leash, 51, 52, 64, 79, 120, 125, 166, 167, 174, 175,
    176, 181, 187, 188, 190, 196, 197, 198, 213
Leash training, 166-167, 197
Leptospirosis, 64, 96, 98, 202
Leptospirosis vaccine, 97
Lhasa Apso, 29, 140, 146
License, 50
Listlessness, 110
Löwchen, 29
Lure coursing, 19, 222
Lyme disease, 99, 101, 204
Lyme disease vaccine, 97, 100

M

Maltese, 28, 140
Manchester Terrier (standard), 27
Manchester Terrier (toy), 28
Manners, 13, 84, 179, 187
Mastiff, 26
Medication, 110, 198, 200
Microchip, 53
Minerals, 128, 129
Miniature Bull Terrier, 27
Miniature Pinscher, 28
Miniature Schnauzer, 27
Mixed-breed dogs, 30-32, 40, 187, 217

N

National Animal Poison Control Center
    (NAPCC), 59, 119
National Association of Dog Obedience
    Instructors (NADOI), 165
National breed club(s), 22, 33, 34, 35, 38
National Council on Pet Population, 37
National kennel club, 65

National registry, 53
Neapolitan Mastiff, 26
Neutering, 34, 37, 104, 105-107
Newfoundland, 24, 26, 94, 204, 205
No command, 176
Non-Sporting Group, 29, 126-127
Non-Sporting Group breeds, 29
Norfolk Terrier, 27, 218
Norwegian Elkhound, 25
Norwich Terrier, 27, 218
Nova Scotia Duck Tolling Retriever, 23
Nutrients, 133
Nutrition, 52, 73, 127, 129

O

Obedience, 13, 19, 30, 31, 41, 46, 47, 65, 182, 212,
    213-214
Obedience commands, 167, 173, 184, 186, 197
Obedience training, 37, 167, 177
Obesity, 125, 137
Old English Sheepdog, 30, 147, 221
Orthopedic Foundation for Animals (OFA), 34
Otterhound, 25
Outside schedule, 156-160
Ownership, 12, 65, 88, 207

P

Papillon, 28
Parainfluenza, 96, 202
Parainfluenza vaccine, 97
Parasites, 93
Parson Russell Terrier, 27, 218
Parvovirus, 96, 98, 202
Parvovirus vaccine, 97
Pedigree, 65

Pekingese, 28
Pembroke Welsh Corgi, 22, 30, 221
PennHip™, 34
Periodontal disease, 112, 113, 147, 148
Personality, 17, 19, 28, 34, 39, 40, 41, 46, 47, 51, 77,
    79, 80, 110, 165
Pet insurance, 95, 99
Pet sitter, 198, 199-200
Petit Basset Griffon Vendéen, 25
Petting, 169
Pharaoh Hound, 25, 222
Physical examination, 50, 112
Pit Bull Terrier, 13
Play, 14, 16, 17, 38, 50, 59, 75, 159, 173, 177
Playing, 13, 55
Pointer, 23, 24, 220
Pointing breeds, 220
Poisoning, 119
Poisonous plants, 56, 59
Police dogs, 26
Polish Lowland Sheepdog, 30
Pomeranian, 28, 94
Poodle, 79, 127, 140, 146
Poodle (miniature), 29, 94
Poodle (standard), 22, 29
Poodle (toy), 29, 94
Porcupine quills, 122
Portuguese Water Dog, 26
Possessiveness, 186
Praise, 82, 153, 155, 166, 167, 168, 169, 170, 172,
    173, 175, 176, 179, 182, 186, 188
Preparation, 49-61
Problem behaviors, 17, 77, 80, 162, 177
    aggression, 31, 34, 46, 76, 78, 82, 83, 85, 86, 87,
    106, 110, 180, 184, 190, 183

barking, 36, 73, 78, 79, 80, 81, 85, 157, 177-179, 185, 190

coprophagia, 186-187

digging, 177, 181

food guarding, 185-186

jumping up, 55, 79, 157, 177, 179

biting, 37, 46, 47, 180-181

running away, 181-182

separation anxiety, 184-185

submissive urination, 186

Progressive retinal atrophy, 34

Protein, 128, 129, 130, 131

Pug, 28, 118, 140

Puli, 30, 221

Puppy Aptitude Test (PAT), 41

Puppy aptitude test, 38, 41

Puppy kindergarten class, 85, 167-176, 213

Puppy kindergarten training, 79

Purebred dogs, 22-30, 40, 65, 187, 209, 217

Q

Quarantine, 65, 197

R

Rabies, 50, 98-99, 202

Rabies certificate, 197

Rabies vaccine, 97, 121, 181

Recall to heel, 175-176

Refusing food, 108

Registration certificate, 65-66

Registration papers, 34

Registry, 65

Rescue group, 38

Respiratory problems, 108

Retriever, 19, 24, 146, 204, 219, 220

Reward(s), 125, 170, 173, 177, 195

Rhodesian Ridgeback, 25, 222

Ringworm, 103

Road trips, 193-195

Rocky Mountain Spotted Fever, 101

Roll over, 172

Rottweiler, 13, 22, 26, 31, 94, 140, 221

Roundworms, 104

Rules, 13, 75, 77, 153

Running away, 181-182

Running eyes, 108

Running nose, 108

S

Saint Bernard, 15, 19, 24, 26, 94, 124, 153

Saluki, 25, 222

Samoyed, 26, 140, 221

Sarcoptic mange, 102

Scenthounds, 25

Schipperke, 29

Schnauzer, 140

Scottish Deerhound, 25, 222

Scottish Terrier, 27, 218

Sealyham Terrier, 27, 218

Search and rescue dogs, 24, 26, 31, 88, 206-207

Seizure, 109, 119

Selecting, 39-48

Selective breeding, 17, 27, 33

Separation anxiety, 184-185

Setter, 24

Shedding, 18, 36, 141, 142

Shelter(s), 17, 31, 36-38, 50, 53, 67, 85, 105, 106

Shetland Sheepdog, 22, 30, 127, 180, 221

Shiba Inu, 29

Shih Tzu, 28, 94, 140, 146, 147

Shock, 117

Showing, 209

Shyness, 34, 76, 86, 187

Siberian Husky, 26

Sighthound, 25, 222

Silky Terrier, 28, 140, 218

Sit, 78, 79, 85, 86, 125, 167, 169-171, 173, 179, 184, 188, 189

Skunks, 122

Skye Terrier, 27, 218

Sled dogs, 26

Smooth Fox Terrier, 27

Snake bite, 121-122

Sneezing, 40

Socialization, 13, 27, 34, 39, 73, 74, 76, 80, 82-87, 167, 183, 184, 206

Soft Coated Wheaten Terrier, 27

Spaniel, 28, 146, 219, 220-221

Spaying, 34, 37, 104, 105-107

Spinone Italiano, 23

Sporting Group, 24, 124

Sporting Group breeds, 23, 24

Sports, 36, 162, 193

Staffordshire Bull Terrier, 27

Standard Schnauzer, 26

Standard, 210

Stay, 167, 171-172, 189, 214

Stool eating, 186-187

Stranger(s), 47, 85, 187, 188

Stripping, 18, 28

Submission, 47, 73, 75, 76

Submissive urination, 186

Supplements, 124, 133

Sussex Spaniel, 23, 221

Swimming, 57

T

Tapeworms, 105

Tattooing, 53

Teeth, 16, 54, 111, 112, 113, 147, 148, 177, 210

Temperament, 22, 23, 31, 34, 38, 39, 40-46, 48, 80, 83, 165, 183, 195, 201, 205, 217

Temperature, 102, 118, 131, 195

Terrier, 140, 218

Terrier Group, 27-28, 126

Terrier Group breeds, 27

Therapy dog(s), 24, 26, 31, 41, 88, 205-206

Tibetan Spaniel, 29

Tibetan Terrier, 29, 140

Tick paralysis, 101

Ticks, 101-102, 104

Time-out, 156, 177, 180

Toenail care, 144-146

Toy(s), 51, 54-55, 59, 82, 100, 155, 159, 179, 180, 181, 186, 197

Toy Fox Terrier, 28

Toy Group, 28, 126

Toy Group breeds, 28

Tracking, 214-215

Trainability, 22, 23, 24, 30, 41, 65

Trainer(s), 46, 87, 152, 158, 163, 165, 169, 181

Training, 11, 13, 27, 38, 47, 51, 67, 73, 74, 80, 86, 125, 187, 189, 205, 207, 216

Training classes, 67, 99

Training problems, 17

Traveling, 13, 53, 193-202

Treat(s), 79, 82, 85, 86, 110, 125, 142, 137, 155, 159, 169, 170, 172, 173, 174, 183, 185, 194

Trimming, 18

U

United States, 129, 197, 200, 212

V

Vaccination(s), 28, 35, 46, 64, 98, 99

Vaccination record, 96

Vaccination schedule, 50, 96, 97

Veterinarian(s), 36, 49, 50, 66, 67, 76, 93, 94, 95, 96, 98, 99, 100, 101, 102, 104, 105, 107, 108, 111, 112, 113, 115, 116, 117, 118, 119, 120, 121, 122, 124, 125, 126, 133, 134, 136, 144, 147, 165, 181, 187, 188, 194, 195, 198, 200, 202

Vitamins, 124, 126, 128, 129

Vitamin supplementation, 66

Vizsla, 23

Volhard, Wendy, 41

Vomiting, 97, 98, 99, 104, 107, 119, 121, 124, 125, 201

W

Walking, 52

Walks, 14, 19, 162, 187, 188, 204

Water, 19, 52, 59, 86, 128, 129, 131, 135, 158, 159, 179, 181, 197

Water bowl, 51-52

Weimaraner, 23, 220

Welsh Springer Spaniel, 23, 221

Welsh Terrier, 27, 218

West Highland White Terrier, 27, 218

Wheezing, 40

Whippet, 25, 222

Whipworms, 104

Wire Fox Terrier, 27

Wirehaired Pointing Griffon, 23, 220

Wire stripping, 140

Wolf pack, 71

Working Group, 26-27, 125-126

Working Group breeds, 26

Worms, 103, 104, 107

Wounds, 109

X

Xoloitzcuintli, 140

Y

Yard, 15, 59, 182, 187

Yorkshire Terrier, 28, 94, 126, 140, 147

Photo Credits

Isabelle Francais

Robert Pearcy

Ron Reagan

Vince Serbin

Photographs courtesy of
American Rescue Dog Association, Foundation for Provided Therapy

Cartoons by Michael Pifer